Strategic Transformation *is a step-by-step guide for transforming the organization for both young and seasoned executives. A must-read for leadership.*

—Bharat Magu, MD, FACP
Chief medical officer, Yuma Regional Medical Center

Juan Riboldi has created a book that skillfully guides leaders through the arduous journey of turning abstract strategic concepts into concrete reality.

Contrary to what many leaders believe, Riboldi's message is that strategy making is much more than a fancy model or a slick matrix. The essence of strategy is putting ideas into practice or, in the words of Helmuth von Moltke the Elder—the celebrated Prussian chief of staff—"strategy is the art of action." Thus, strategy really begins when the rubber meets the road.

The library shelves are loaded with books on strategy formulation but good books on strategy execution are rare, and this book will surely become the definitive go-to book for any leader who has an interest in the subject.

—Dr. Eitan Shamir
Author, Transforming Command

Juan Riboldi is a visionary leader for implementing successful change. Strategic Transformation *is a focused guide to making meaningful and lasting change in an ever-changing world. Juan hits the nail on the head time and time again in this insightful journey. This book is for doers!*

—Rob Holcombe
Director, Conferences and Workshops, BYU Continuing Education

In 2019, the Frederick Community College Mid-Atlantic Center for Emergency Management and Public Safety expanded. The expansion brought disparate academic programs together to form a highly functional team. As the executive director, I led the newly formed team using the five principles for mastering change as outlined in Juan's first book, The Path of Ascent. In spite of the surreal time in human history with a global pandemic, national economic distress, and social and civil tensions, the first-year anniversary on July 1, 2020, found the team realizing much success.

As I continue to lead the center into its second year in a world that is complex, interdependent, and interconnected, I am enthusiastic to apply the framework in Juan's new book, Strategic Transformation, to turn decisions into results. Strategic Transformation provides the core framework that recognizes the complexities of the world we work and lead in today and establishes a progressive operating model that is decisive, agile, and creates value for a wide variety of organizations.

—Kathy L. Francis, MS, CEM, MDPEMP
Executive director, Frederick Community College Mid-Atlantic Center
for Emergency Management & Public Safety

The concepts in this book are important and relevant especially in light of the current situation. Juan has a unique ability to take complex ideas and break them into simple and easily implemented steps. Strategic Transformation helped me see clearly how value is created and how results are achieved through Juan's process of strategy development, deployment, and execution. I've worked with Juan both as a consultant and as the COO of my company. He practices what he preaches—delivering value. This book is full of real world examples that help bring home the concepts so you can instantly see how you can implement the concept in your organization. His generous use of graphics really brings the ideas forward and makes them easy to understand and remember. I'm sure you'll get real value from this book.

—Russ Gentner
CEO, Listen Technologies

Juan Riboldi knows what he is talking about. Juan has both significant experience and the successful ability to help executives and team members apply easily understood principles and practices for effective strategic transformation. He was successful with a prior company I worked for and I have since seen him successfully lead many other companies to industry-leading value creation. This is a must-read for anyone wanting a road map to greater value creation in this ever-changing business world.

—Daron M. Jones
President and COO, TractusMed

All I can say is "Wow." I've used the concepts of Juan Riboldi's first book, Path of Ascent, successfully to transform organizations for many years. So I was very excited when I found out he was writing another. Strategic Transformation did not disappoint. There are many business books written and published each year, but seldom can you read them and put them to immediate use. Like Path of Ascent before it, Strategic Transformation is the exception. In this book, Juan sets forth a clear path through the uncertainties of today's world and outlines the concepts and processes used to jump-start the creativity and potential of organizations, communities, and people. It's clearly the best book for *harnessing, leveraging, and applying every ounce of potential within your organization, your community, and yourself.* Strategic Transformation *is a must-read for anyone looking to transform their environment!*

—Don Francis
Director of human resources, City of Hagerstown, Maryland;
Washington, DC, Metro Area
Adjunct professor, Mount St. Mary's University

Strategic Transformation *is an excellent book with real-life situations giving leaders a fresh perspective on best practices to successfully implement strategic transformation and change management.*

—Sultan Altobieb
Change management program GD
Minister's advisor, MOMRA, Kingdom of Saudi Arabia

STRATEGIC
TRANSFORMATION
HOW TO DELIVER WHAT MATTERS MOST

STRATEGIC
TRANSFORMATION
HOW TO DELIVER WHAT MATTERS MOST

JUAN RIBOLDI

Advantage.

Published by Advantage, Charleston, South Carolina.
Member of Advantage Media Group.

ADVANTAGE is a registered trademark, and the Advantage colophon is a trademark of Advantage Media Group, Inc.

Printed in the United States of America.

10 9 8 7 6 5 4 3 2 1

ISBN: 978-1-64225-138-8
LCCN: 2020915782

Book design by Mary Hamilton.

This publication is designed to provide accurate and authoritative information in regard to the subject matter covered. It is sold with the understanding that the publisher is not engaged in rendering legal, accounting, or other professional services. If legal advice or other expert assistance is required, the services of a competent professional person should be sought.

Advantage Media Group is proud to be a part of the Tree Neutral® program. Tree Neutral offsets the number of trees consumed in the production and printing of this book by taking proactive steps such as planting trees in direct proportion to the number of trees used to print books. To learn more about Tree Neutral, please visit **www.treeneutral.com**.

Advantage Media Group is a publisher of business, self-improvement, and professional development books and online learning. We help entrepreneurs, business leaders, and professionals share their Stories, Passion, and Knowledge to help others Learn & Grow. Do you have a manuscript or book idea that you would like us to consider for publishing? Please visit **advantagefamily.com** or call **1.866.775.1696**.

*To everyone striving to create
meaningful value through their work.*

CONTENTS

FOREWORD

As an entrepreneur and business owner, you hope to cross paths with an individual like Juan Riboldi. I've known Juan for almost four years, since my business partner and I first hired him as a consultant for many different business ventures. We hired Juan to help with our strategy for raising some capital necessary for growth. Juan quickly went to work finding the best-case options for us. He was able to not only assist on a partner buyout but also secure additional capital for us without going to a private equity or venture capital firm. With Juan's invaluable aid, our business has grown over 1,600 percent from 2017 to 2019.

Juan is a thought leader focused on optimizing organizations to create value for their customers. He is the founder of a strategic consultancy firm called Ascent Advisor and has consulted with C-level and executive teams at Fidelity, IBM, the *Financial Times*, Sony, and many others around the world. If that isn't impressive enough, Juan is currently consulting with the Kingdom of Saudi Arabia on a government transformation project that includes several ministries. And he has taught executive courses at Harvard Business School, Pepperdine University, and Brigham Young University.

Over these last few years, it has been exciting to work with Juan as we develop new strategies and continue to transform our businesses. Juan provided the framework that has enabled us to transform our business into a long-term value creator. His unique, systematic approach to strategy and innovation is why his results are always positive. He conveys a simple message linking change to opportunity.

Leading one of the fastest-growing companies in the United States has given me practical appreciation for the unique challenges and opportunities inherent in rapid change. Delivering innovative solutions requires the ability to be both creative and practical. At Dynamic Blending Specialists, we strive to deliver greater value and better solutions than what is usually expected in our industry, while providing rigorous operational efficiency and product quality. Mastering these complementary values is critical to becoming a transformational leader.

The main reason you should read this book is because you, like most other business leaders, probably realize that strategic transformation requires more than innovation. It requires visionary and pragmatic leadership at every level of the organization. Incorporating these values into your organization's culture is at the core of achieving sustainable success.

Some companies still disregard the principles Jim Collins taught in the best-selling book, *Good to Great*. They are unwilling to transform and innovate, despite proven frameworks and principles for growth. The risks are too much to handle for many leaders. They think that getting into the slow lane of innovation is sufficient. But, in fact, as Juan points out, the greater risk is to become less relevant by failing to innovate.

The amazing thing about this book is that it addresses a broad range of leaders, from start-up entrepreneurs to executives at well-established corporations to government officials seeking to innovate. Juan's writing is helpfully technical where it needs to be and makes conceptualizing his approach simple. With this book, you will come to understand what is required to execute a successful strategic transformation that creates lasting value.

Many of the large Fortune 500 companies have gone through the strategic transformation process, and the organizations that have flourished are those that truly seized the opportunity to transform themselves. Take Amazon, for example. Anyone attending college in the early 2000s most likely bought some textbooks from Amazon. I know I did; it saved me a lot of money! Back then, Amazon was already a successful online used bookseller. But what if Jeff Bezos never had the vision to drive for more value? If Amazon had not undergone several strategic transformations, it would not be the world's most valuable brand today.

The hard reality is that, in today's business world, organizations require a higher level of strategy and innovation to survive. Unless organizations start to transform how they drive value, they will be caught in Jim Collins's "Doom Loop." They must lay the groundwork for long-term success, instead of opting to find the quick short-term profit. Every leader needs to treat strategic transformation as essential to remaining competitive and attaining ultimate success.

Mastering the Strategic Transformation Framework in this book should be an essential part of every executive's and entrepreneur's approach to leading change. These principles will guide leaders through a well-executed and dynamic transformation. Every leader should read this book, familiarize themselves with the framework, and apply these concepts in their own organizations to realize their most important goals.

The business landscape is getting increasingly more competitive every passing day. Uncertainty is high. Companies that fail to transform, even if they were once successful, quickly lose ground or cease to exist. Change is inevitable, but transformation is a deliberate choice.

I would like to end with my favorite quote by Peter Drucker: "The best way to predict the future is to create it."

I hope you enjoy this book. Cheers.

—Jordan Erskine,
Cofounder and President, Dynamic Blending Specialists

CHAPTER ONE

DELIVERING WHAT MATTERS MOST

S trategic transformation is how leaders turn vision into results. How can you play a critical role in creating value in today's uncertain times?

The world is changing fast. We are required to change with the times to remain relevant. But merely adapting to the new conditions is insufficient for success. In order to succeed, we are required to reinvent ourselves, reposition our organizations, and reimagine what we do. We need to strategically transform ourselves and our organizations.

Whether you are launching an innovative start-up, repositioning a striving business for growth, leading a large corporation through industry disruption, or navigating social and economic change in the public sector, you need to deliver what matters most—to you, to your team, to your organization, and to society at large.

Strategic transformation follows predictable patterns that if correctly applied will lead you and your organization to value creation. Strategic transformation is about value creation.

Those who are able to implement the new direction with speed, clarity, and precision gain an edge, while those who become paralyzed, reactionary, or confused will stumble or fail. At your work and in your personal life, how you respond to change determines your chances for success.

Strategic transformation points the way forward during times of uncertainty and risk. The examples of transformational leadership in our times are many. Consider the leadership vision that inspired a nation to send a man to the moon. Tap into the practices that gave Google incremental learning advantages to gain search engine dominance. Consider the massive focus that allowed a team to locate and rescue thirty-three mine workers trapped two thousand feet underground under intense time constraints. Learn how fast-food restaurant managers engage ordinary hourly workers to deliver extraordinary customer service and record profits. Let's review the practices that propelled Intel to deliver breakthrough innovation to become one of the world's most valued enterprises.

Learning about the most successful strategic transformations of the last decades reveals a consistent pattern that, if applied correctly, will give you and your organization the confidence to reach your goals. This book explains the principles, practices, and tools you need to make the most relevant things happen.

Behind every decisive victory, every remarkable achievement, every significant advance, there is a strategic transformation. Without it, your greatest aspirations remain unrealized dreams, and your diligent work amounts to pointless labor. We look for strategic transformational leaders, yet too few demonstrate the qualities of such a leader. We expect to see it in successful organizations, but it shines through only occasionally. When it does, however, great things happen.

Trying to realize the most powerful dreams or solve the most painful problems—for ourselves, for our businesses, and for our communities—can become frustratingly difficult. It's easy to run into obstacles, but much harder to find effective ways to overcome those obstacles. It's easier to tell others what they need to do, but much harder to get them to do it right. It is the rare person who can grasp what is going on in a complex situation, focus on the most critical opportunities, and take decisive and competent action to realize their goals.

But you don't need to possess rare intuition or unusual amounts of raw talent. You just need to know what to do. As I have advised leaders through the strategic transformation process, I have gained a distinct understanding of what it takes to deliver critical results. By applying the principles and practices described in this book, you, too, can become a strategic transformational leader.

MASTERING DECISIVE MOVES

The amphibious landing was thought to be impossible. There were no beaches, only seawalls. Troops, equipment, and supplies would have to scale sheer cliff walls at night and be positioned by early dawn. Approaching vessels would have to maneuver around shallow rocks and shoals. Tidal currents ran as high as eight knots. The waters approaching the little bay were most likely mined. A small island fortification would have to be captured before proceeding to the landing spot. Any disabled or sunken ship could block the passage, spelling disaster for the entire operation.

Worst perhaps were the tides, fluctuating about thirty-two feet, which except at high tide would turn the bay into a muddy flat. All this could be accomplished on just a few specific dates and within a two-hour period on those dates, when there was sufficient depth for an amphibious assault. But, if successful, before sunrise the enemy would be surrounded and suddenly forced to fight on two fronts. Because this approach was entirely unexpected and nearly impossible, it could be the masterful, decisive move that presaged overall victory.

Yet all of Douglas MacArthur's generals and advisors were unconvinced. They wanted to land more troops near Busan, where the UN forces had been pinned down by the best North Korean troops. They believed this was a more realistic and feasible strategy. But MacArthur knew it was a strategy that would cost more casualties and prolong the war. Instead, he envisioned a much more complex and ultimately far more effective move. Landing at Inchon, deep behind enemy lines, near the captured capital of Seoul, would deal the North Korean army a conclusive psychological blow.

One general and advisor after another warned MacArthur about the dangers of landing at Inchon. MacArthur openly acknowledged the complexity of the operation. Then he proceeded to explain to the doubters that the disadvantages of Inchon as a place to stage an amphibious landing were precisely what would enable UN troops to surprise and defeat the North Koreans.

MacArthur deftly deflected the alternatives, saying that even a successful landing elsewhere would not defeat the enemy but only maintain the status quo. Admiral Sherman, who had been sent by the Pentagon to dissuade MacArthur from his plan, became a major ally after hearing MacArthur's eloquent and convincing defense of his surprise attack plan. This critical political ally turned the tide in his favor with others, and MacArthur's plan was approved.

With the buy-in from those above and below him, MacArthur proceeded to orchestrate the transformation of his war strategy with great precision, trapping the North Korean army between his troops in Busan and those he landed at Inchon and creating panic in the enemy ranks. The North Korean army, which had occupied South Korea for three months, was gone within fifteen days of the Inchon landing. It was one of the greatest strategy transformations in military history.

A leader's abilities are put to the test when they are faced with situations where there are high stakes, conflicting views, and critical consequences. Success hinges on the capacity to execute on what is usually more difficult but critically needed. Leaders like MacArthur have been able to excel in such situations by mastering a set of complementary skills and practices. The strategic transformational leader is able to:

- Conceptualize a way to accomplish seemingly impossible goals

- Recognize the real and perceived difficulties as solvable challenges

- Present the plan to achieve a meaningful result with clarity and conviction

- Build a core team of allies to help instill confidence in followers and win support from skeptics

- Carefully plan for the practical, logistical requirements for successful transformation

- Mobilize resources to act swiftly and decisively when it's time for action

- Keep open lines of communication during the transformation to adjust and adapt as needed

Some of the most successful organizations demonstrate these abilities as they strive to lead their industry, differentiate themselves from competitors, and succeed in the face of stiff challenges. As we'll see in the following section, this approach is what led Intel to become one of the most valued companies in the world.

INNOVATION BY DESIGN

Andy Grove, the CEO of Intel, demonstrated all of those strategic transformational leadership abilities and more in his own drive to differentiate his company and succeed in the face of stiff competition.

Intel was involved in its own "war" in the 1990s. It was competing with many microprocessor producers for a growing electronic communications market that was hungry for more and faster computing power. Big names such as Motorola, IBM, Apple, AMD, Toshiba, National Semiconductor, and Hitachi, to name a few, were all after the same market. Grove knew that in order to win against such strong competition, Intel would need to perfect every aspect of strategic transformation, from the design to the production, distribution, and marketing of microchips.

To achieve that goal, Grove asked his managers to push the envelope in every direction. Managers received wide latitude to experiment and be innovative, but they had to measure their performance every step of the way. From the design of microprocessors to the marketing campaigns to the way they conducted management meetings, Grove insisted on constant improvement in every business process.

Perhaps most important, Grove engineered an organization capable of producing a continuous flow of radical innovation. The complex designs that accounted for the speed of Intel's chips went through a competitive process that was far fiercer than any of their competitors had.

Intel set up competing engineering teams to vie for the next breakthrough. Every quarter the teams' designs were rigorously evaluated and compared against each other. Through a strict peer review process, only the best designs were accepted. Those designs were also infused with the useful ideas of engineers from the teams whose designs didn't advance, and those engineers were moved to the winning teams. This kept all of the engineers in the race, engaged and contributing to the ultimate chip's design.

Going from a field of sixteen competing teams to eight, four, two, and finally down to one, everyone crossed the finish line a winner, bringing their best ideas to the production of the next best product to hit the market—products that continually amazed and baffled Intel's competitors.

But, long before the new, winning chip was proclaimed as the best in market, Intel engineering teams were already hard at work on its successor. They were back in their competing teams vying for the next innovative breakthrough.

Grove also insisted that his managers measure every aspect of their performance. They were given latitude to experiment and try new things, as long as they were able to learn from their experiences. In order to integrate innovation and discipline, Grove demanded precise measurement and analysis.

Grove also pushed operational capacity beyond foreseeable needs. To excel in manufacturing, Intel invested millions of dollars in plants that could crank out more processors in a day than some rivals could build in an entire year. Through manufacturing precision and automation, Intel's chips became not only the fastest but also the cheapest to produce.

The chief engineer of Intel competitor National Semiconductor once plopped a plastic bag full of National's low-cost memory chips onto his desk, in front of me, while holding in his other hand an Intel microprocessor. He said, "The challenge is that Intel can produce this one chip for about the same cost that we can produce any one of these chips, but because of the circuitry design alone, we sell our chips by the pound, while Intel sells each one of these at a premium."

In the end, it was not that Intel's strategy was significantly different from that of its many powerful competitors—Intel simply executed its strategy significantly better. With greater vision and focus, wider engagement and more disciplined processes and measurement than any of its competitors, the organization achieved disruptive innovation. During this period, Intel became one of the most valued companies in the world financially, as a place to work, and as a source for world-changing technological breakthroughs.

THE POWER OF STRATEGIC TRANSFORMATION

Intel's capacity to deliver breakthrough innovation every eighteen months demonstrates powerful strategic transformation. All of Intel's competitors had essentially similar capabilities, products, and customers. But Intel figured out how to outperform in a way that made them increasingly superior. Often, the most successful companies are not unique in their offerings, markets, strategies, or people, but in their ability to deploy their resources better than others.

Strategic transformation is the ability to match a great strategic vision with flawless implementation to realize their combined full potential. You can have a brilliant strategy—even an A+ strategy— but poorly executed, it will only deliver C results, barely a passing grade. A great strategy poorly executed is a missed opportunity. An OK strategy—let's say a C strategy coupled with a great implementation will still deliver at least B results. But in the long run, the faithful execution of a poor strategy will yield increasingly poorer results. The ideal scenario is to match a brilliant strategy with great execution to deliver A+ results—great ideas well implemented is what is required for a strategic transformation.

The Value of STRATEGY + EXECUTION	Great Strategy	Poor Strategy
Great Execution	A+	B
Poor Execution	C	D

Figure 1.1

Strategic transformation relates to emerging and widespread business concepts in the fields of strategic innovation, technology disruption, agility, continuous improvement, change management, and business acceleration. All of these concepts define specific approaches for implementing change. Strategic transformation focuses on adopting best practices and innovative technologies to build a highly competitive organization by optimizing human performance.

Strategic transformation provides a proven framework that leverages the best qualities of multiple approaches with the flexibility to adapt to a given situation. Whether an organization needs to transform into a target state, accelerate the execution of a set direction, or become more nimble and agile at responding to emerging trends, strategy transformation outlines the principles, process, and practices necessary for success.

Moreover, while most organizational change methodologies address only the organizational level, strategic transformation connects the organizational, team, and individual levels. The role of individual leaders and team members in leading, promoting, and adopting a strategic change is just as critical, if not more important, than the strategies, structures, and processes that need to be put in place.

In the end, all organizational change amounts to collective change in individuals. The choice each person makes ultimately determines what gets done and how it gets done. The cumulative effect of individual values, attitudes, behaviors, and practices ultimately results in the organization's culture. So, a successful strategic implementation needs to address individuals and teams as much as the organization at large.

For the leader responsible for strategic transformation, this requires the ability to think, plan, and act at all these levels, focusing on broad organizational strategies, structures, processes, and resources while at the same time paying attention to the aspirations, capabilities, motives, and incentives of the individuals assigned to carry out such initiatives. The strategic leader needs to develop an ambidextrous skill set to be effective and authentic at the organizational and individual levels. The strategic leader needs to:

1. Be both visionary and pragmatic

2. Align to leadership directions and lead others with confidence

3. Build strong relationships of trust and hold those people accountable for results

4. Foster innovation and initiative and set rigorous processes and practices

5. Celebrate wins and successes and evaluate performance objectively

Not an easy task, yet critically important in order to be both strategic and practical. So how can anyone become the kind of ambidextrous leader capable of strategic transformation? It starts with a simple choice. When faced with a change—the kind that makes us wonder how in the world we can possibly handle it—those who can seize the situation as an opportunity ultimately succeed. Those who become stuck seeing what is happening as a threat are likely to fail. At work and in our individual lives, our ability to frame change as an opportunity determines our ability to master the situation and succeed.

Change is inevitable, but growth is entirely optional. To fuel economic recovery and attain success, leaders need to reinvent their organizations around creating value. Any business can be positioned as a growth business if you are willing to rethink your strategy.

REFRAMING CHANGE AS OPPORTUNITY

"We don't have a role for you in this organization," my manager told me. I was shocked. Over the previous year, I had led two successful product launches and frequently received positive recognition from that manager and many associates. The morale on the team I led was high, and we were on a roll. Why was this happening to me?

I had joined IBM while I was still completing college. After an initial round of positions in software development, and as I started graduate business school, I was promoted to managing two struggling education product lines that had been in development for too long, delayed by numerous redesigns and recurring bugs. If the products couldn't be satisfactorily released relatively soon, the entire operation would be shut down.

As a young and energetic employee, I accepted this challenge. It was my first real taste of management—at one of the best companies in the world. What I didn't realize was that I had been put in charge of a sinking ship, a group of products for which the company had little hope. But with the help of a savvy IBM mentor who had led turn-arounds, we were able to resolve the issues that were holding up these products. It was a valuable first experience. Within a year, the team had managed to release both products, which earned award-winning recognition, leading IBM to invest in the site and expand the product lines.

While I was still savoring the success of my team's accomplishment, IBM decided to restructure the operations and bring a more experienced product manager into my position. I was told that there was no longer a position for me on the team. I felt betrayed. My mentor recommended me for a research role at IBM's New York head office. That still didn't feel good, because I was living with my young family in Utah! I didn't know how to respond to this sudden and unexpected change.

When we perceive that change is happening to us, we tend to place a red frame around it. In a red frame of mind, we see change as a negative event, a threat or even a defeat. It's not useful to remain in a red frame of mind. The red frame keeps us stuck in a victim role.

If we want to lead change rather than become a victim of it, we need to choose a more productive point of view. Putting a green frame around the situation helps us see opportunities. When we adopt a green frame of mind, we see change as an opportunity for growth, learning, advancement, clarity, and ultimate success. The green frame allows us to respond more effectively to the situation.

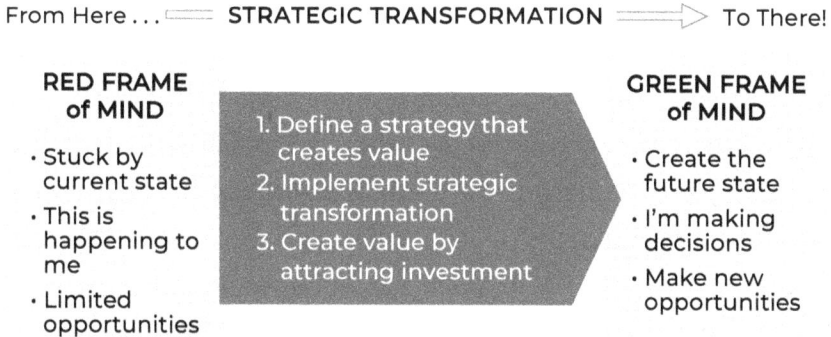

From Here... STRATEGIC TRANSFORMATION To There!

RED FRAME of MIND

- Stuck by current state
- This is happening to me
- Limited opportunities

1. Define a strategy that creates value
2. Implement strategic transformation
3. Create value by attracting investment

GREEN FRAME of MIND

- Create the future state
- I'm making decisions
- Make new opportunities

Figure 1.2

Focusing on what you can do about the situation rather than on what you can't do gets you back into growth mode. While change is inevitable, growth is a choice, an intentional decision to learn, advance, and benefit from a given situation.

While change is inevitable, growth is a choice, an intentional decision to learn, advance, and benefit from a given situation.

The five steps to shift our frame of mind from reactive to proactive are:

1. State the change objectively—what is happening

2. Identify ways you can influence the situation

3. Accept what you cannot change

4. Change what you can make better

5. Define for yourself and others the opportunity

Back to my situation at IBM, after some deep soul searching I was able to put myself in a green frame of mind. I decided to accept the research position in New York, even though, at the time, it seemed like a big, uncomfortable hassle. The adjustment to living and working in the new environment proved very difficult for a long while. But in the end, it turned out to be a great opportunity. Working at IBM's global headquarters as a business analyst with an elite team of IBM consultants, I ended up learning a lot about how IBM went about implementing one of the most critical strategic changes in its history. And ultimately I found a profession that I loved, which has been my career for the last thirty years.

Had I remained in the red frame of mind, I would have missed out on the opportunity of a lifetime. Adopting a red or a green frame of mind is simply a choice. The red frame keeps us stuck in a victim role, paralyzed by fear and doubt. The green frame allows us to respond more effectively to situations. The impact on ourselves and others is tremendous.

* * *

This book is based on personal experiences I've had and practical insights I've gained over the last thirty years. I've been engaged in a fruitful professional career advising innovative leaders at some of the best corporations and fastest-growing enterprises on their most critical decisions. Throughout these busy years, my focus has been on delivering successful strategic transformation.

This book is also the result of extensive original research in addition to rich personal experience from studying public and private organizations that experienced significant strategic change over the last ten years. By comparing the decisions and outcomes of the companies that succeeded with the ones that failed, I reveal in this book the principles and practices for making strategic transformations work.

In the following chapters, you will learn how to lead strategic transformation for your organization. You will glean the ideas, decisions, and practices that helped other leaders and organizations achieve extraordinary results, even in the face of great difficulties, uncertainties, and challenges. In the next chapter, you will learn about the conceptual framework and core elements of a successful strategic transformation.

KEY TAKEAWAYS

- Strategic transformation is how leadership decisions are implemented by the organization to achieve a critical result.
- Without strategic transformation—the capacity to turn vision into reality—the best plans remain unrealized dreams.
- Masters of strategic transformation:
  - Conceptualize a way to accomplish seemingly impossible goals
  - Recognize the real and perceived difficulties as solvable challenges
  - Present the plan to achieve a meaningful result with clarity and conviction
  - Build a core team of allies to help instill confidence in followers and win support from skeptics
  - Carefully plan for the practical, logistical requirements for successful transformation
  - Mobilize resources to act swiftly and decisively when it's time for action

- ▫ Keep open lines of communication during transformation to adjust and adapt as needed
- Success isn't necessarily tied to exciting, original concepts; it can also be tied to good, simple ideas that are very well executed.
- Most strategies fail or falter in the execution stage. Effective execution of a transformation is at least as critical as the strategy.
- Strategic transformation requires an ambidextrous skill set, the ability to work at the organizational and individual levels.
- Strategic transformation requires leaders to be both visionary and pragmatic, to simultaneously foster innovation and initiative, while instilling discipline, focus, and accountability.
- Successful strategic transformation requires the ability to recognize the change as an opportunity, to make it your own.

C H A P T E R   T W O

FRAMEWORK— TURNING DECISIONS INTO RESULTS

Strategic transformation is how you, as a leader, can get bold, innovative ideas effectively implemented.

Some individuals can come up with brilliant ideas, but that doesn't necessarily mean they can successfully make them happen. Some people are better at conceptualizing an innovative vision. Others are good at getting things done, following clear directions. Few, however, can do both. These individuals have mastered the ambidextrous qualities of the transformational leader, who can execute on what is strategically critical.

This chapter describes how you can become a transformational leader who can deliver what is most critical. You can accomplish this by leveraging the combined qualities of diverse people playing key roles and following the strategic transformation process. This chapter explains how to seize present opportunities and turn them into consistent outcomes in today's economic environment.

Strategic transformation is more important than ever in today's fast-paced, high-stakes, unpredictable environment. Market opportunities evolve rapidly, favoring dynamic responses. Seemingly simple decisions in one area have far-reaching impact on multiple unforeseen areas. Faulty planning or poor execution can quickly escalate into a crisis. A leader's ability to make sound decisions and implement them effectively marks the difference between winning and losing.

To excel at strategic transformation, you need to put all the pieces together in the right place and sequence. You need to inspire others with a shared vision, set clear priorities, align resources, and deploy the right people to engage in effective processes and practices that deliver critical results. All these steps, when properly followed, will deliver success even in difficult situations. Strategic transformation is a process that you can master.

* * *

From the air-conditioned office high on the top floor of the skyscraper, you could see, through the glass walls, the entire city flanking the balmy sea and spreading far into the hot desert. It was an impressive sight of magnificent towers and busy highways gleaming brightly in the sun, as if defying the harsh and inhospitable surroundings. The scene was even more spectacular when considering that only a few decades before, what is now Dubai was a fledgling trading seaport teeming with vendors living in tents and traveling on camels.

"That's where it all started!" said the city officer, pointing toward Deira, at the mouth of the Dubai Creek, where remnants of the old town barely remain. "Our grandfather had a vision. He thought of using his wealth to turn the town into a world trade center by attracting foreign investment into the region." He was obviously proud of his tribal heritage and the vision that transformed his Bedouin society into today's super-modern hub for international business.

"We've been building on that same vision for the last three generations," he said, looking at the pictures of the crown rulers of the United Arab Emirates in his office. It is obvious that the sheikhs' vision had accomplished much. He went on to tell me about the many struggles they had to overcome to build a thriving city on the sand.

As we both contemplated the scenic view of present-day Dubai, he turned my attention to the future. "This is our unfolding vision!" he said as he removed a curtain from one of the office walls, revealing a mural depicting a Dubai extending far beyond its current boundaries. "We need help to build this."

Before oil was discovered, Dubai was a desert outpost relying on the trade of pearls, silk, and fish for sustenance. Since the 1970s, the oil industry has fueled the economy, propelling several transformations to make it a renowned world destination for business and tourism. The incredible speed of this development, coupled with the ambition of Dubai's vision, have amazed the world. Dubai has achieved this success through smart, bold, and innovative strategic thinking.

Dubai's success is attributed to capable, visionary leaders and their determination to bring their vision into reality. The foundation behind what Dubai has become is the farsighted and level-headed policies pursued by the late Sheikh Rashid and his successor, Sheikh Mohammad. In the early days of Dubai's expansion, they were often seen driving around the city, checking that it was clean and well-kept. They were notorious for paying surprise visits to various development projects to ensure that those projects were making steady progress, talking with the workers and reporting on what they saw to the people in charge.

The rapid pace of sustained growth, coupled with over-reliance on oil, has brought new challenges to the bustling city. Diversifying the economy will require increased openness, greater market innovation, and deregulation of the private sector. How are Dubai's leaders responding to these challenges? A bold, long-term vision coupled with clear strategic planning and a determined execution of the transformation are still the driving forces for overcoming the current challenges and embracing a hopeful future. Dubai's rise from a fledgling seaport to a renowned world trade center has been, and continues to be, vision driven.

THE STRATEGIC TRANSFORMATION FRAMEWORK

THE CORE

Strategy is real time. So is the execution of a transformation. Each informs the other. At the core, the relentless focus is on driving value for customers, employees, and investors. Looking from the inside out, strategic transformation is about creating value. This simple and yet critical component is often missing or vaguely defined. Strategic transformation is centered on creating value, which needs to be defined and measured from the start. Success depends on aligning to that core.

Since driving value is at the core, it needs to be defined first, not last. It is the most critical component to the success of the entire process. When aiming for a defined and measurable goal from the start, the entire strategic transformation aligns all activities to the desired outcomes. As a result, the outcomes are more likely to be achieved. When the core is missing or is secondary to the strategic transformation process itself, people may go through the motions without delivering an outcome.

Strategic transformation is not about following a methodology or applying a process as much as it is about achieving a desired result. The end result can be measured in multiple ways. For some organizations, driving value is best defined in financial, operational, cultural, or customer gains. The following are a few examples.

Strategic transformation is not about following a methodology or applying a process as much as it is about achieving a desired result.

The leadership team of a US federal government agency, foreseeing the need to become more efficient, innovative, and responsive to market trends, set as one of their priorities developing capacity to lead change. This agency developed cadres of high-performing individuals to act as champions for change, facilitating various cultural and process improvements. The driving value continues to be measured in terms of leadership capabilities.

The management of a global manufacturing corporation saw a need for increased operating income through operational improvements in on-time delivery, product quality, and safety. Their strategic initiatives have been focused on driving operating income through on-time delivery, product quality, and safety.

The executive team of a fast-growing technology company recognized that innovation was the driver for success in their industry. Their rapid transformation from an ambitious start-up to an industry leader required relentless focus on innovation fueled by attracting top talent, fostering a culture of innovation, and tackling challenging projects, even at the expense of sales or profits.

THE FOUR PHASES

Looking from outside in, the strategic transformation process consists of four consecutive and interdependent phases: strategy, deployment, execution, and results.

Strategy sets the vision and direction. Deployment aligns resources to the strategy—individual people and the whole organization. Execution puts in place the processes and practices to achieve operational gains, which in turn delivers results by measuring performance, recognizing wins and reporting accomplishments.

The traditional strategic planning and execution process that most consultants offer ends with deployment, leaving it up to the client to make the operating model work and deliver results. If results don't materialize, it's because the client did not implement the model correctly. This is quite convenient. A different set of consultants may come in at the back end to make things work, which often run counter to the original strategy and deployed organization. So the operational improvements are not transformative or sustainable in nature.

We advocate instead for an integrated approach that aligns the strategy, people, organization, processes, practices, and measurements from start to end. This comprehensive approach increases accountability, as it places responsibility for success with the same group of people throughout the entire process.

Often, the entire process is presented as lengthy and laborious. Some companies have accepted that the strategic transformation can only take place over a period of two to three years. Most modern organizations can ill afford working on a two- or three-year fixed strategic plan. The world evolves quickly. Even a one-year set of initiatives may not remain relevant through the full twelve months!

The strategic transformation cycle offers instead an agile approach to planning, deploying, implementing, and evaluating. This happens in real time and across multiple fronts in response to emerging realities. Through quarterly reviews, the Strategic Transformation Framework requires course checkpoints and, if needed, course corrections. These recurring cycles of planning and execution help calibrate direction while building momentum for regular wins.

The four phases are sequential, cyclical, and iterative. Each phase informs the other. Each phase feeds off the previous one. For example, the strategy feeds off existing results and informs the organizational structure, while the deployment is best guided by strategic priorities that influence people, processes, and practices.

At a glance, the four phases for strategic transformation are as follows:

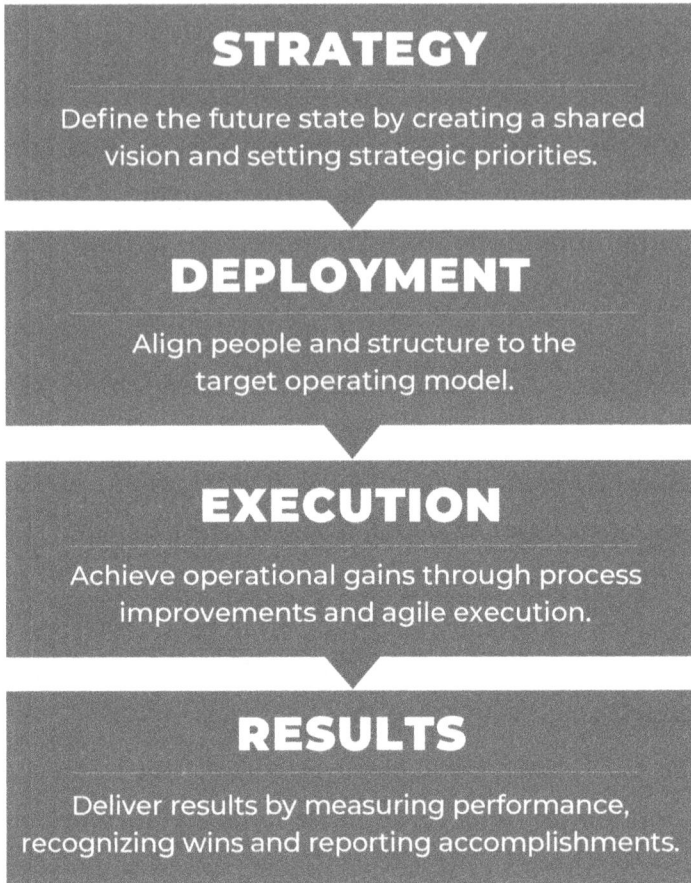

STRATEGY

Define the future state by creating a shared vision and setting strategic priorities.

DEPLOYMENT

Align people and structure to the target operating model.

EXECUTION

Achieve operational gains through process improvements and agile execution.

RESULTS

Deliver results by measuring performance, recognizing wins and reporting accomplishments.

Figure 2.1

THE KEY COMPONENTS

Completing the Strategic Transformation Framework are the key components within each of the four phases. There are eight key components in total around the core to drive value. Each key component is essential to a successful strategic transformation, as each delivers a unique and distinctive value.

When a key component is present at the right time and in the right sequence, it accelerates and reinforces the overall strategic change. When a key component is missing or undermined, there are foreseeable setbacks and predictable failures down the road.

The Strategic Transformation Framework is represented as a cycle depicting the evolving nature of change. The cycle can be seen as a single independent cycle or as a series of interdependent cycles playing out concurrently at various levels. For example, an organization pursuing a sweeping transformation can be applying a comprehensive eighteen-month strategic transformation cycle while deploying strategic initiatives using the same process in six-month cycles and having high-impact projects completed within one hundred-day cycles.

The following Strategic Transformation Framework illustrates the four phases, the core, and the eight key components as a cyclical process.

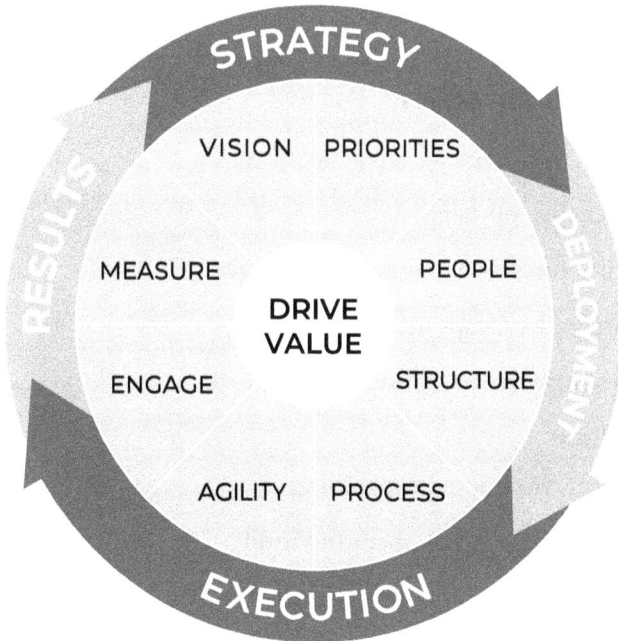

Figure 2.2

PHASE 1: STRATEGY

Vision

- Assess internal situation
- Map stakeholder support
- Benchmark best practices
- Envision future state
- Identify transformation targets

Priorities

- Identify strategic priorities
- Set goals and objectives
- Outline strategic initiatives
- Define success measures
- Create action plan

PHASE 2: DEPLOYMENT

People

- Identify top talent
- Hire or develop core competencies
- Assign key responsibilities
- Activate the transition plan

Structure

- Assess functional capabilities
- Define the target operating model
- Design the organizational structure
- Identify roles and responsibilities

PHASE 3: EXECUTION

Process

- Identify operational targets
- Streamline work processes
- Develop tools and templates
- Automate through technology

Agility

- Adopt an agile mindset
- Implement agile practices
- Accelerate project execution
- Monitor and report early wins

PHASE 4: RESULTS

Engage

- Define the desired culture
- Identify and model key behaviors
- Train and coach on key behaviors
- Recognize success stories

Measure

- Focus on goal achievement
- Identify and measure KPIs
- Monitor and analyze performance
- Target and report big wins

Aligning individuals across the organization to drive value through a series of strategic actions requires leadership, commitment, and coordination. This creates the need for three distinct roles during strategic transformation: one for setting directions, another for engaging the people, and a third for coordinating the project.

ROLES

Top-heavy initiatives, where change is mandated from the senior leaders, lack engagement at the lower levels. Employee-focused initiatives lacking a measurable strategic impact are not sustainable. Successful change requires aligning leadership vision and direction with individuals' commitment and participation. There is also the need for a third group to align and coordinate both, resulting in the following key roles.

The Strategy Team sets the strategic direction and makes the key decisions to guide the transformation. The Transformation Team acts as the program manager for overseeing, and communicating the work plan, schedules, activities, deliverables, and progress reports. The Activation Team is a cross-functional group, representative of the groups affected by the strategic change, assigned to work in pairs with specific groups outside of their own to make transformational improvements.

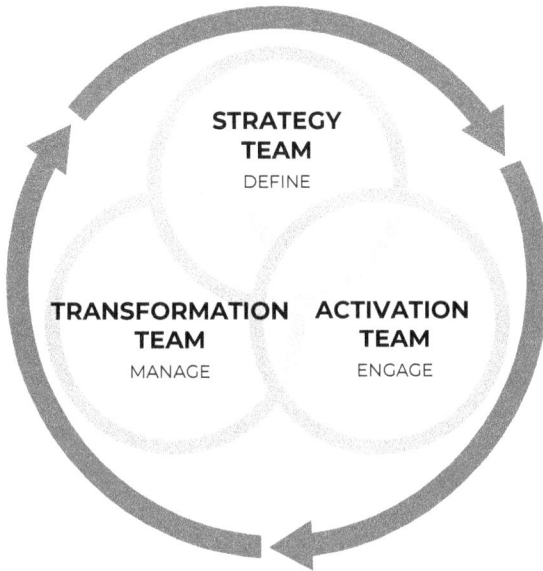

Figure 2.3

The Strategy Team consists of the executives leading strategic change. Their role is to set the strategic direction, oversee the deployment, monitor the execution of the transformation, and evaluate the results. Their combined skill set requires them as a group to be visionary and pragmatic, engaging and disciplined. It is particularly helpful when at least one of the strategic transformation leaders has previous experience or natural aptitude for leading change.

This group needs to be kept relatively small and select, usually comprising one to three executives. Occasionally, this group may expand temporarily to include other senior executives as needed to inform and enlist support from the entire organization. The role of this group is not to initiate change directly through their chain of command. This is where the Activation Team comes in.

The Activation Team represents a cross section of the organization from all the areas affected by the strategic change. The members of this team are selected for their aptitude to influence change. They are high-potential rising stars and opinion leaders who are willing to go the extra mile. They are nominated and invited by the Strategy Team to lead strategic initiatives as part of the Activation Team for a defined period of time. Their commitment usually requires them to dedicate approximately ten hours a month over a twelve-month period.

Their different backgrounds ensure different perspectives, views, and attitudes toward the strategic change—which also means that at least some individuals will initially hold critical or opposing views on the strategic direction. This ensures that all voices and views are fairly represented, and that the opposition is engaged from the start. Interestingly, these challengers usually become instrumental converts who help influence others about the strategic plan's viability.

The Activation Team needs to be empowered with training, tools, visibility within the organization, and recognition by the leaders. The team's primary task is getting everyone to participate in the strategic change. They are deployed in pairs or trios to assigned areas of the organization outside the area in which they usually work. This ensures that they don't have to deal with the prejudices they might face in their usual environment. It also fosters greater objectivity, credibility, and learning, as they are exposed to areas they were not previously familiar with.

The members of the Activation Team usually put in significant time in this role, but they often find it the most exciting part of their work, as they experience opportunities for leading strategic initiatives, making real change happen, and even achieving career breakthroughs.

The Transformation Team consists of specialized internal and external resources who provide project management, subject-matter expertise, process oversight, and change management. Their role is to coordinate the strategic transformation process end to end, interacting with the other groups and, if needed, with individuals and teams across the organization.

The Transformation Team needs to be well organized and highly credible at managing the project with precision, good communication, and confidentiality. For all or most of the members of the Transformation Team, this role becomes their only or main assignment for the duration of the strategic change. This requires that provisions are made in advance for their career advancement once their assignment is completed.

When I am involved as a **strategic advisor**, I play a role in each of the three teams. I work with the executives on the strategy and coach them in their roles as strategic leaders. I also help to define, train, and coach the Activation Team members in their assignments, as well as being an active participant in the Transformation Team, lending expertise, process oversight, and project coordination.

PUTTING IT ALL TOGETHER

"I felt we had plateaued," said Jim Phillips, CEO of Digital Gateway (DGI). For seven consecutive years, DGI had been one of the fastest-growing companies, receiving consecutive awards for growth and innovation. Jim led the company from start-up to becoming the software automation leader in the office equipment industry.

Then, with DGI at the top of their game, conditions changed. A new economic climate stalled DGI's growth, and it started to decline.

Years of success and profitability had resulted in a growing list of strategic projects, creating a massive lack of focus. The original vision that once guided the company had become blurred by myriad initiatives. Accustomed to a dominant position, the company's culture had lost its original sense of urgency. People became entitled and a culture of low accountability set in.

This realization hit home as DGI's management team attended an executive briefing I was hosting. When I asked the audience to state their company's strategy in thirty words or less, no one from DGI was able to do it. No single statement was even possible. All I could get as an answer from DGI's management team was a long list of over thirty strategic initiatives. Jim realized that something had to change. To meet the challenge, he brought in my team as strategic advisors to spur rapid improvements.

Over the next two quarters, DGI was to shift into a higher gear, turning a downward trend into a record year. This change required engaging all employees in the strategic transformation process. During an initial assessment, employees identified strengths and areas for improvement. The collection of inputs from employees were posted on an open area wall which became known as the Wall of Improvements. To drive these rapid improvements, they created an Activation Team of change champions representing formal and informal leaders in the organization.

Over the years, friction had crept in between departments, to the point where many were no longer feeling like one team. To build a common purpose, DGI engaged teams across the organization to create and present stories of success. This culminated in an envisioning event where all company employees shared in an ambitious vision of the future in which DGI became the undisputed industry leader. DGI's vision became a rallying point for employees and managers alike.

With a clear vision in mind, DGI's management team quickly regained their focus and set clear priorities. At this point, Jim helped refocus on measurable goals, which the company started tracking on a weekly basis.

What became known as the "Locker Room" was a weekly stand-up meeting where the management team reported the current status against their department's goal. People stood in a semicircle facing a whiteboard filled with weekly, monthly, and quarterly performance measures. Reporting on goal achievement amidst peer cheering and friendly hissing, DGI's management team bonded around ambitious strategic goals.

As people began to see what was possible, they started investing in their work, often going beyond the expected. The customer support group stepped up service, leading to more and increasingly better customer interactions. The technology development team became more reliable at meeting their deadlines. Sales was inspired to start hitting their goals without excuses, which led to them even surpassing what initially seemed like impossibly high targets.

DGI leaders received coaching on their style and were required to formally assess their talent pool. The talent assessment led to getting the right people in key roles. Toward the end of the first one hundred days, DGI was once again a highly focused and well-performing company. The capstone was taking the discipline of the Locker Room to every department and individual, setting and tracking performance indicators weekly.

DGI's management team streamlined their processes, gaining clarity around what work mattered most and eliminating what was not critical. Through regular data-driven progress review meetings, managers were able to make better decisions. This led to operational improvements that increased customer loyalty and profitability.

Within two quarters, by year end, DGI delivered a record year in revenue, surpassing their original sales goal and overshooting their annual projections by 25 percent! Beyond the impressive success in financial performance, DGI was transformed in a more significant way. The culture regained the belief in their ability to do great things. They had increased their capacity and unity as one team. More importantly, they became convinced they could realize their vision, which materialized in the following year as they acquired their two main competitors in the industry and became the undisputed leader.

* * *

Now that you have an overall understanding of the Strategic Transformation Framework, I'll present greater detail about each of the four phases and eight key components in the rest of the book, which is structured as follows:

Part one (chapters 1 and 2) introduces the Strategic Transformation Framework as a concept with practical applications and its core focus, four phases and key components as well as the required roles.

Part two (chapters 3 through 10) describes in detail the four main phases and the eight key components for achieving strategic transformation, with practical application examples.

Part three (chapters 11 and 12) shows how leaders can activate the strategic execution of a transformation to deliver what matters most for them as individuals and for the organizations they lead.

Strategic Transformation outlines a proven process that will make it possible for you to take your organization to the next level. As a leader, you need to create value, quickly and reliably. Strategic transformation is how you can accomplish that more predictably and successfully.

Change is inevitable. It's happening all around us at an accelerated rate. Growth is optional. It is a choice that you and others can make. Strategic transformation is how to influence a change for the better.

KEY TAKEAWAYS

- Strategic transformation is how plans made by decision-makers get executed effectively by their teams.

- Strategic transformation is a process that, when properly followed, delivers great value to individuals and organizations.

- To excel at strategic transformation, you need to inspire others with a shared vision, set clear priorities, align resources, and deploy the right people to adopt effective processes and practices that deliver critical results.

- The Strategic Transformation Framework includes four phases:

    1. Strategy

    2. Deployment

    3. Execution

    4. Results

- Within the four phases, there is a core component focusing on driving value to a specific and measurable goal.

- Supporting the strategic transformation process, there are eight key components that focus on driving value to customers, shareholders, and associates:

    1. Vision

    2. Priorities

    3. Structure

    4. People

    5. Process

    6. Practices

    7. Engage

    8. Measure

- There are three groups required for strategic transformation, playing three distinct roles. One for setting direction, another for engaging people, and a third for coordinating the project:
    1. Strategy team
    2. Transformation team
    3. Activation team

- Working with all three groups is the strategic advisor.
- Strategic transformation is how to influence a change for the better.

CHAPTER THREE

VISION—CREATING THE STORY OF SUCCESS

ision is action on the belief of what we can become.

Everything now in existence was first conceived as a vision in our mind's eye. Vision is an expression of the willpower to materialize things not yet in existence. Vision turns what is initially unimaginable into what becomes possible, then probable, and finally inevitable. It inspires action and sustains it over time. Vision is the power to influence the future.

We all have a vision. But unless we turn vision into a powerful force to trigger action, it may never become reality. The ultimate power of a vision is in the intent. Is the vision self-centered or is it for the greater good? As we focus on others' needs to address broader interests, we overcome divisions and distrust and instead build common purpose. Most visions fail to inspire others simply because they are self-centered. A powerful vision inspires others with a cause greater than themselves.

Storytelling is how we communicate a vision. Ever since humans first gathered around a fire, they have told stories to share important information, to convey values and pass on traditions. Good stories capture people's imagination—they create a vision of what is meaningful and possible.

Transformational leaders share their vision by telling stories of future success as if they had already happened. The story of success creates a script for the transformation. We are the script writers of our lives. We may even use modern means to capture, edit, and post our stories. What story of success are you telling? What is your story of success?

Transformational leaders share their vision by telling stories of future success as if they had already happened.

---

* * *

One day in 1983, Steve Jobs walked into a meeting at Apple headquarters carrying a conspicuous plastic bag. He opened it and slid onto the conference table a flat object that looked like a beige desk diary. All eyes were fixed on the strange object. No one knew what it was. They probably suspected it was another prototype for their feedback—maybe a portable keyboard or a hard drive to enhance their existing computer.

But what happened next was totally unexpected. The strange object had hinges on one side, and Jobs opened it like a book. One half was a keyboard, the other half was a computer monitor—but unlike a monitor, it was perfectly flat.[1]

"This is my dream of what we'll be making in the mid to late 80s," Jobs told his bemused colleagues. "We won't reach this on Mac One or Mac Two, but it *will be* Mac Three. This will be the culmination of all this Mac stuff."[2] With help from his leading designers, Jobs was showing his colleagues the future—an easily portable, user-friendly personal computer. "Even though Steve didn't draw any of the lines, his ideas and inspiration taught us how to design today's laptop. We didn't know what it meant for a computer to be 'friendly' until Steve told us."[3]

Eight years later, in 1991, Apple introduced the PowerBook, a revolutionary notebook PC that weighed about five pounds. It wasn't the first laptop on the market, but it was clearly the best—more user friendly than anything out there at the time. Jobs had infected Apple with his vision for the future. This led to a revolutionary product that changed the computing world.

Steve Jobs was not the inventor of the portable computer, but he had a clear vision of its potential. He envisioned a tool that would enable any individual in the world to unleash their creativity anywhere, anytime. It was this vision that made the PowerBook such a huge success.

When he put it out, Jobs didn't just announce a new, innovative product. He announced a revolution of thought. Apple's memorable invitation to all of us was simply to "Think Different." He shared his own inspiring vision with us.

---

1   Cruikshank, Jeffrey L. 2006. *The Apple Way.* New York: McGraw-Hill.

2   Moritz, M. 1984. *The Little Kingdom: The Private Story of Apple Computer.* New York: William Morrow.

3   "History of Computer Design," www.landsnail.com/apple/local/design/design.html.

"Here's to the crazy ones, the misfits, the rebels, the trouble-makers, the round pegs in the square holes … the ones who see things differently—they're not fond of rules … You can quote them, disagree with them, glorify or vilify them, but the only thing you can't do is ignore them, because they change things … they push the human race forward, and while some may see them as the crazy ones, we see genius, because the ones who are crazy enough to think that they can change the world, are the ones who do."

Almost overnight, the Apple PowerBook became the best-selling computer in the United States, with $1 billion in sales in its first year. THAT is the power of vision.

VISION CREATES PURPOSE

A powerful vision inspires others with a cause greater than themselves.

An innovative leader like Steve Jobs may have had a powerful vision, but in order to make that vision real, many others had to adopt it as their own. Many others needed to be inspired by it and to work together to make it happen. Otherwise, the leader's vision goes unrealized.

We enlist others' commitment by helping them become part of the vision. It has to be their journey and their success as well. This requires bold and worthwhile goals. These aren't just stretch goals; they're not even just very ambitious goals; they are goals that challenge people to leave their comfort zones and take a leap of faith.

As people become a part of accomplishing something great and meaningful, they commit fully. They overcome divisions and distrust to join forces for a common purpose. Purpose binds people to a cause greater than themselves.

This is how President John F. Kennedy rallied an entire nation to regain a leadership role. The US space program was struggling and lagging behind the USSR's steadier achievements in space travel. Each failed rocket launch further undermined the national confidence.

In May 1961, Kennedy gave a speech before a concerned Congress to address the state of the Cold War with the USSR. He ended his speech by unexpectedly challenging the nation with a goal: "I believe that this nation should commit itself to achieving the goal, before this decade is out, of landing a man on the moon and returning him safely to the earth. … If we make this judgment in the affirmative, it will not be one man going to the moon, it will be an entire nation. For all of us must work to put him there." He ended his speech with the inspiring and challenging statement, "We choose to go to the moon in this decade and do the other things, not because they are easy, but because they are hard."

Sending a man to the moon was far beyond anything anyone had ever accomplished in space at that time. For most people, it was literally inconceivable. But, for that very reason, it excited the imagination. Committing to this vision created a rallying point for the entire nation. A huge number of people had to buy into this vision and work tirelessly to make it a reality—and they did.

Within eight years, man walked on the moon, and Kennedy's unifying vision brought the US closer to fulfilling its leadership mission in the world. THAT is the power of vision.

* * *

What does a powerful vision look like? How do you create a vision that inspires everyone in your organization? What can you do to help others commit to the vision?

In order to capture the imagination and inspire people to work toward a common purpose, a vision should have the following characteristics:

- It is not true now.

- It requires seeing something that does not exist now *as if* it is already in existence.

- It is more than just incremental steps.

- It is something big, something that represents your organization's greatest aspirational goals.

- You can almost see it in your mind.

- It is such a vivid description of the future that "you can almost taste it."

- It represents a great purpose, beyond self-interest.

- It is an inspirational story of success that makes people want to help achieve it.

- It is an aspirational view of the future state.

- It is a guiding star that inspires people and guides an organization toward a future which it can aspire to.

As a leader guiding an organization through strategic transformation, keep these characteristics in mind. In order to help others commit to the vision, get them involved in creating it. The envisioning process becomes even more important than the actual vision statement.

A vision becomes most critical when there is low trust. The signs of low trust are groups blaming each other, frequent turf battles, and suspicion of hidden agendas. In such situations, a shared vision can become a powerful way to align people to a common purpose. The vision creates a focal point for people to overcome their differences and join forces in support of a common cause.

HOW TO CREATE A POWERFUL VISION

People are much more likely to retain and work toward a vision that they helped create.

People are much more likely to retain and work toward a vision that they helped create.

While strategic leaders can state the vision, it is critical to engage many others in becoming a part of that vision by helping create it. The Activation Team plays a key role in facilitating an envisioning process that involves everyone across the organization. The following exercises will assist the Activation Team in the vision-creation process.

1. Design thinking

2. Mind mapping

3. Envisioning

4. Storytelling

5. MVP prototyping

We'll describe how each exercise can be facilitated and what each can accomplish. Each exercise will be illustrated by a real-life example of vision creation for the city of Provo, Utah, at a time when it was competing for the Google award to become a gigacity.

Google invited five cities across the US to participate in a contest for a grant resulting in seven years of high-speed internet access and related fiber-optic services free of charge to the residents; the winner would be the city that could produce the most compelling case for using this advanced technology to transform their economy, education, and community. By delivering an inspiring vision, Provo, Utah, was awarded Google's high-tech infrastructure and became a gigacity.

DESIGN THINKING

Design thinking starts by gaining an in-depth understanding of who your customer is and what that customer wants—or doesn't want. Not just in relation to your product or service, but, even more broadly, what they want and need *in their life*—what moves them, motivates them, excites them, and dissatisfies them. This helps you think more holistically about the customer.

With your customer in mind, ask participants to define the main challenges that the customer is currently facing and brainstorm possible conceptual solutions to those problems. Express the solutions not as specific initiatives, but as creative approaches for how to deal with such problems. Test the approaches out to refine the ideas. Once participants have a sound understanding of the ideas, vote on the most promising ideas.

Design thinking helps identify high-level ideas to address broad needs and wants of the customer. These solutions generate a series of high-level concepts that can be expressed as going from the current state (problem) to a target state (solution).

In the Provo gigacity project, I started by meeting with the city mayor and the chief administrative officer to discuss their vision for Provo and what Google Fiber could do for the city. To frame the conversation, we identified customer segments that the city of Provo was focused on serving. These included groups such as working families, university students, business entrepreneurs, healthcare providers, people with outdoor/sports lifestyles, the elderly, and underprivileged groups.

We discussed who these groups represented, their demographics, situations, needs, and wants. We paid special attention to what Provo was currently offering and would ideally be able to offer to each group with Google Fiber. This resulted in a set of statements describing opportunities for each customer segment.

For example, Provo could boost entrepreneurship by designating an area for economic development, a start-up village offering free high-speed internet and related services. This framework allowed us to start planning the next step in the vision-creation process by involving various stakeholder groups.

MIND MAPPING

Mind mapping is designed to link the high-level ideas from the design thinking step with a process for evolving such ideas through stakeholder input. Mind mapping exercises can be facilitated in small or large groups. Participants are given as a starting point the high-level ideas from the design thinking stage. This allows them to understand the scope of the vision.

Then you ask participants to describe what specific ideas come to mind when they think of the proposed vision. They are required to write each individual idea separately in a card and post each card on a wall. This quickly builds up to a wall of ideas.

Once all the ideas are on the wall, invite the participants to come to the wall and read what everyone wrote and to group the cards by theme. When working with large groups, this may require several rounds of people to read and group ideas by theme. This results in groups of cards representing the main themes and subthemes.

Complete the mind mapping exercise by associating the themes and subthemes, showing the relationships. Organize the ideas around the central concept and radiating out from the center in a spider web pattern. This expands the design thinking concepts into a more comprehensive mind map.

For the Provo gigacity project, we decided to invite representatives from the different customer segments to a half-day event at the Provo Library. We had approximately fifty people in all. The mayor kicked off the event with a description of what Google Fiber could mean to each group and to Provo city as a whole. His remarks made reference to the ideas from the design thinking conversation.

Then we facilitated the mind mapping exercise, which resulted in an impressive wall of ideas, ranging from simple and practical concepts to creative and innovative proposals. All ideas were welcomed! We invited groups of ten to fifteen people to come to the wall to read and group them by theme, creating associations between core themes and subthemes. When the exercise was completed, we had an impressive collection of grouped ideas.

What was needed next was to bring this collection of ideas into a cohesive vision through the envisioning exercise.

ENVISIONING

Envisioning is a creative visualization exercise. You can practice envisioning as an individual or facilitate it for small groups of people.

When working with large groups, it is best to organize smaller subgroups of five to eight people.

You start by picturing yourself in the future. You can state an actual year or date in the future. Ask participants to imagine themselves at that future date and the amazing success already accomplished by then. They can close their eyes and fully envision in vivid detail what it is like to have accomplished the vision that's been laid out—what it looks like, how it worked, what we did, how people are using it, and what's remarkable about it.

People should get to the point where they can see this future in their mind's eye so believably that it seems real. It is important to stay grounded in the future date. It is a trip to the future! Then ask participants to describe what they envisioned as things that have already happened.

In the Provo gigacity project, we worked in round tables of five to eight people, each individual visualizing new services, experiences, functions, and practices in the various sectors they represented. Then they were to describe to their peers what they envisioned, as if these things were fully accomplished. Finally, we asked each table to select a spokesperson to deliver a thirty-second story narrative of their envisioned state.

STORYTELLING

Storytelling is the way to present the envisioned stories. People can work in groups to consolidate their ideas and write down the story of the future as clearly and vividly as they can. To add a sense of intensity to the presentation, announce the storytelling as a contest, where each spokesperson is representing a team. The spokesperson presents their story in a creative way, as if making an announcement in a newspaper, magazine, or TV interview. But they have to condense the entire presentation to only thirty seconds!

When the groups are ready to present, which is usually within ten minutes, you can conduct the storytelling contest. Each group tells the story its own inventive way. Applause is for every presenter and the group chooses a winner, or multiple winners by categories, such as most innovative, best delivery, or most practical.

In the Provo gigacity project, groups worked at their tables to draft creative, imaginative, and often humorous stories of Provo's future as a gigacity. A group of outdoor advocates, for example, presented a map of Provo linking all the parks and recreation areas with a continuous biking and running path, including a professionally designed mountain biking course and streaming live posts and videos of group rides that enthusiasts could follow, like, and join. Another group, healthcare professionals and university students, came up with an "Ask a Nurse" online service, giving local university students quick healthcare advice for the common health issues they face without them needing to spend time and money on more expensive doctor visits.

Some stories made us laugh, some piqued our interest, and some truly inspired us. Awards were liberally given for the best stories, and in the end we had an emerging picture of what a Provo gigacity could be like. Now we were ready to capture, share, and promote this emerging vision through prototyping.

PROTOTYPING

Prototyping delivers a graphic or physical representation of the minimum viable envisioned product or service that can be shared as a report, posted to generate engagement, or experienced as a test concept. Depending on the objectives, prototyping can be a facilitated group exercise or simply built as a quick production project. The approach depends on the intended uses.

I have seen a variety of applications, from high-end video productions that helped raise investment capital for the vision to corporate intranet blog posts that generate input and engagement across an organization to graphic visualizations created live to communicate the vision during a strategic retreat. In some cases, the vision-creation process resulted in prototyping an envisioned product or store concept to test the vision.

In the case of the Provo gigacity, we deployed five project teams to evolve the main envisioned ideas. One of them resulted in a closer partnership between entrepreneurs, real estate developers, banks, and the university to evolve a start-up village. Reclaiming a neglected area of the city and turning it into a start-up hub, with high-tech infrastructure and high-speed public transportation, the start-up village attracted entrepreneurial activity.

When Provo city actually won the gigacity grant, several additional projects received the support needed to materialize, including the biking trail with the professional mountain biking track.

* * *

The vision-creation exercises can be used independent of each other to generate quick creative insights or in sequential order to create a strong, unifying narrative vision of the future. The compelling story of success will inspire people across an organization with a common purpose. Let's look at how a strong vision unexpectedly helped unify and transform an organization.

WHERE'S THE BEEF?

When Michael, the CEO and founder of a successful meatpacking company, saw "developing a vision" on the agenda for the company retreat I was going to lead, he said, "We don't need vision. Just focus on the strategy."

Michael was a pragmatic business leader of one of the largest producers of meat patties in the US. He was a self-made man from Chicago who saw little value in spending executive team time discussing the company's vision. Management was not going after a mighty cause; they were not trying to disrupt the industry.

"It's all about tonnage," the operations VP explained to me at the retreat. "All we need is to add an additional three to five hundred tons of meat to the production plan." That would provide a substantial gain in their share of the beef production market.

Naturally, I tried to persuade him that establishing a vision was important, but he wasn't convinced. Given the type of business, I recognized the need for a more pragmatic focus on things such as expanding existing accounts, winning new accounts, improving operational efficiency, and maintaining safety and quality standards while meeting financial forecasts for the next year.

The strategic retreat delivered what was expected. As a management team, they reviewed their customers, discussed the industry, set goals for the next year, and walked away with a solid action plan. The mood was bold and confident. It was just a matter of execution—we thought.

Flash forward a year, when we reconvened for the next strategic planning retreat. This time, Michael wanted to expand the agenda and add more in-depth market analysis, deepen conversations using strategic thinking models, and develop a more detailed action plan.

The reason he wanted to try these new approaches was that, while the company had continued to grow, it had not fully achieved its business goals. After a very productive couple of days, we walked away from the retreat with clear goals and a detailed action plan. But there was still something missing.

As the following year entered its final quarter, we all recognized that, even though the team had worked really hard and the company was still growing, the year's goals were not going to be achieved. Michael wasn't satisfied.

This time, at Michael's request, vision was on the agenda. "We need to catch the vision of why we are going after these goals," said Michael as we outlined the meeting agenda. During the retreat, the team participated in exercises intended to create a shared vision for the company. The task proved more difficult than initially expected.

Even after hours of rich conversations, creative brainstorming, and insightful ideas, the management team wasn't any closer to describing the company's vision. At one point I turned to Michael and asked him to share his vision for the company. All eyes turned to him. A long pause followed as Michael wrestled with something deeply held inside himself.

To encourage him, I said, "Knowing all the sacrifices you have made over so many years to build this company, I'm sure you have a driving purpose. Would you share that with us?"

Michael started talking about his childhood, about growing up in a rough Chicago neighborhood with few means and often insufficient access to food. He saw that the kids who ate well grew up strong, could defend themselves, could go to school, and had a chance to break free from poverty.

Michael went on to say, "But even if you had the chance to attend school, you still needed sufficient protein to think clearly and do well in school. A hamburger a day was all that a kid like me needed to grow strong, get an education, and do well in life." The founder and president of one of the largest food producers in the US was confessing to his management team that he knew firsthand the meaning of poverty. They listened quietly and respectfully.

Finally, he said, "At one point, I resolved that if I ever did well, I would want to make sure that every kid had the chance to eat a hamburger a day. The protein is what gives them a chance to grow strong, to learn something, to make a better future for themselves. So, when the opportunity came in my life to buy a meat producing company, I immediately went for it, committing myself to providing affordable protein to as many kids as possible."

I had never heard anyone talk about the purpose of providing low-cost meat in these terms. It was moving and inspiring—and I knew instantly that this was the vision, the greater purpose, that Michael needed to share with his whole company. As soon as his management team heard this story—including his own son, in charge of sales, who did not know this part of his father's history—they knew that what had been missing was, "Why are we doing this? What is the bigger purpose?"

Once they heard Michael's story, everyone in the company felt a new sense of purpose. The operations manager said, "The campaign of rolling down the vision to the folks was one of the most powerful forms of training we could have ever done." They finally understood why they were doing what they were doing.

The line workers took in this vision and were highly motivated by it and improved their productivity—even the unions saw a higher purpose in the work and were more reasonable in their demands. The sales people went after clients with renewed energy. Everyone wanted to realize Michael's vision, to get more protein out into the world at a price that anyone, including poorer kids' families, could afford.

They entered new markets boldly, because they wanted to expand their ability to reach those kids. They also rejected new non-protein products that some competitors were moving into, because it didn't fit with their mission.

Suddenly, this company knew its purpose, and the results demonstrated that. All of the production and sales goals that had seemed unattainable for two years were met and exceeded over the next year. THAT is the power of vision!

THE POWER OF A PERSONAL VISION

The principles of strategic transformation can be applied to an individual life as well as to organizations. A story of my own vision quest demonstrates how this applies to finding purpose in life.

In the first chapter, I described how I became a part of a business consulting team at IBM's world headquarters in Armonk, New York. I was with one of the top companies in the world, I was making good money, my wife and I had had our first child—everything looked great! But somehow, I didn't feel fulfilled.

I was living in Connecticut at the time and commuting daily to Armonk with a group of IBM managers. Listening to them talk, I learned what my life at IBM would look like ten or twenty years down the road, if I stayed on that track. I was privy to the nature of the work, the difficulties, the rewards, and all of the other aspects of corporate life at IBM headquarters.

I was aspiring for more from my work. But I didn't know how to point myself in the right direction. One day, my wife suggested that I take the next weekend off from everything and really spend time figuring out what I wanted to do, what I would really enjoy doing, and what I wanted for the rest of my life. In short, she was telling me to create a vision for myself.

So I did. I went off to a secluded Connecticut forest by Candle-wood Lake. It was a nice, quiet area where I could concentrate. At first I just sat there with a pad of paper and a pen, not sure what to do. Finally I said a silent prayer asking for direction and guidance. Then I drew a long line across a sheet of paper and started putting tick marks for each of the next ten years, from 1990 to 2000. By then I would be thirty-five years of age. And I thought, *What do I want to be doing by the time I'm thirty-five?*

What came to mind immediately was having a consulting business. I pictured myself traveling around the country, even internationally, working with business executives. I imagined myself advising senior leaders on topics that at that point in my career were only the domain of the very senior level consultants and executives I saw walking the corridors of IBM headquarters. I pictured myself being the person who came in from the outside and offered insights, ideas, and advice. That picture was very appealing to me.

I wrote down some keywords and phrases that came to mind—for example, "traveling around the country," "international travel," "strategic advisor to executives," and so on.

I even pictured where my family would live. I drew a house overlooking a lake with some very large mountains in the backdrop. Somehow, the picture looked very natural and appealing, and it was completely different from my current surroundings. I realized that I was to move back to Provo, Utah.

As I immersed myself in that picture and in those words and phrases, I thought, *Okay, if this is true, what needs to happen between now and then to help me get there?*

I started doing a little bit of logical reverse engineering. I marked years when four children would be born. I identified steps for leveraging the experience I was getting at IBM to join a consulting firm. I put a date for each step on the timeline I had drawn. On January 1997, I wrote "start your own consulting firm." I called it Decision-Wise, for the ability to make wise decisions. I continued filling out my timeline with dates for various accomplishments, and by the time I was done I had envisioned the whole next decade and knew what I was to do.

And the amazing thing is, things pretty much happened as I'd predicted they would—when I'd finish my MBA, when I'd get a job with a consulting firm, even, in January 1997, when I'd start my own consulting firm! I founded DecisionWise (yes, even the name was what I'd originally envisioned it to be), the company became a success, and, after ten years, my partner bought out my interest in it—and it still exists. THAT is the power of vision!

* * *

The power and importance of creating a vision for your organization can't be overemphasized. Building a common purpose is critical to aligning people's minds, hearts, and hands to achieve the strategic implementation of a plan. People need to understand the why before they commit to the what. When people have been part of creating your organization's shared vision, they will feel that the plan is their own. The story of success you create will act as a guide to the future you've envisioned.

KEY TAKEAWAYS

- Vision is the willpower to materialize things not yet in existence. Everything now in existence was first conceived as a vision in our mind's eye.

- A powerful vision inspires others with a cause greater than themselves. We enlist others' commitment by helping them become part of the vision.

- A strong vision should have the following characteristics:
  - It is not true now.
  - It is more than just incremental steps.
  - You can almost see it in your mind.
  - It represents a great purpose, beyond self-interest.
  - It is a journey more than a destination.

- A shared vision can overcome a lack of trust, a lack of purpose, and internal organizational conflict. It aligns everyone in the organization behind a common purpose.

- The vision-creation exercises that I have found powerful and effective are:
  - Design thinking
  - Mind mapping
  - Envisioning
  - Storytelling
  - Prototyping

- Just like an organization, individuals can apply the same practices to create a vision of their future.

CHAPTER FOUR

PRIORITIES— ACHIEVING CLARITY BY WORKING SMART

Strategic transformation requires both purpose and focus. Vision brings purpose. Priorities provide the focus.

Clarity around priorities allows us to focus on what matters most. Lack of focus causes people to go after whatever seems urgent at the time. Most individuals and organizations attempt to do too much. As a result, the most critical things don't get done right. The most effective leaders instead stay focused on what matters most by working smart.

In today's work environment, most of us are constantly juggling an increasing amount of work. Piled upon that are numerous shifting priorities and expanding expectations. Good, responsible, hard-working people usually respond to the escalating workload with a simple strategy: do more.

Clarity around priorities allows us to focus on what matters most.

The do more strategy requires that we work harder. This usually means spending more time at work, taking fewer breaks, creating extensive to-do lists and checking things off as they get done. Those attempting to do everything on their plate take many hits. But it doesn't stop there; the problem propagates.

The greater problem with the do more approach is that it perpetuates reactionary work. When we are not focused, we cause many others to be unfocused. Reactionary work makes people busy doing things of questionable value. The lack of focus inherent in reactionary work is a main cause of why smart people and successful organizations do dumb things.

Instead of allowing reactionary work to dictate what you do and have others do, we advocate for a different approach: work smart. To work smart you need to regularly assess, adjust, and deliver on the most critical priorities.

Observe the most effective leaders. Despite what goes on around them, despite the complexity of the task at hand and time pressure, the most effective leaders stay focused on getting the most critical things done. They filter the noise, renegotiate expectations, respond deliberately, and mobilize others to do what should be done.

To work smart, you need focus. With focus you concentrate your energies and those of others on the most critical priorities. You use your time and the time of others on the most relevant things.

What happens with all the other stuff? It gets deprioritized. It's either done later, delegated to others, or not done at all. Surprisingly, those things that are eliminated are never missed. Prioritization increases the value and influence we have in an organization.

* * *

André Sougarret had to figure out how to work smart. And he had to do it fast!

In only a few critical days, he had to mobilize hundreds of people representing multiple disciplines from various countries and working for different organizations. The task at hand was complex and unprecedented. He was appointed by Chile's president to assemble and lead the rescue of thirty-three miners trapped two thousand feet underground in a collapsed mine in the Atacama Desert.

Despite the urgency of the situation, Sougarret and his team knew that they needed to make sound decisions. A wrong decision could cost precious hours or days and kill the miners. When Sougarret first got to the mine site, it was a chaotic aggregation of people and equipment. He quickly brought organization and focus to the situation.

One of the first things the teams realized was that getting food and water to the miners could be accomplished quicker than getting them out and would buy time to find the best rescue solution. So the initial, clear priority was to locate and connect with the miners so they could receive life-sustaining supplies. This effort took seventeen arduous days of continuous trial and error drilling deep into the mine. Faced with uncertainty as to their location, success depended on fast learning cycles. And, eventually, they succeeded.

Concurrently with the effort to deliver food, another rescue operation focused on finding a way to get the miners out once they were found. Teams of experts from around the world started working on the best methods to drill a rescue hole. Teams pursued plans A, B, and C in parallel. The three alternative approaches offered a rational basis for deciding which method would prove most promising.

While the rescue attempt was going on, Sougarret did his best to insulate his team from the media, the miners' families, and any other curiosity seekers who showed up at the site. He understood that, with time being of the essence, the team needed to be free of distractions and able to focus solely on their tasks.

Finally, on day sixty-five—the longest time any miners had ever been trapped underground—a drill broke through to the shelter, and four days later all of the thirty-three miners had been brought to the surface, dazed and in some cases ill, but all alive! It was the greatest rescue in mining history. It could have only been accomplished with leadership that brought a clear focus to doing the right tasks at the right time.

DEFINING THE STRATEGY

Most leaders spend significant time crafting strategies to accomplish their goals. Yet few individuals can clearly state their organization's strategy. Despite the amount of resources allocated to strategic analysis, formulation, and planning, most companies don't really have a strategy.

If you ask a group of senior leaders to write down, in thirty words or less, the organization's strategy, you are likely to get inconsistent answers. Some statements will resemble the company's vision. Others will describe specific initiatives. Some will simply focus on a success measure such as financial performance. While all these elements are important, they are not a strategy.

Boiled down to its essence, a strategy is a game plan to achieve a goal by a set date. The game plan is intended to describe the means by which the goal is to be accomplished.

To better understand the value of each element in the strategy, let's consider what a strategy statement might look like. The examples of strategy statements shown in the graph illustrate how each of the three elements adds a unique value to a complete strategy statement. Take away any one of these elements and the strategy is incomplete.

Strategy =	Goal	+	Date	+	Game Plan
Our business strategy is to generate	**$100 M** in global revenues		by the year **2025**		through **direct sales + acquisitions**
Our marketing strategy is to reach	**100 K** FB social media followers		within the first **90 Days**		through daily **posts + comments**

Figure 4.1

The goal by itself is too vague. Setting a target date for accomplishing the goal provides accountability. The game plan informs us how such a goal is to be achieved. When all three elements of the strategic statement come together, we have a plan for achieving a time-bound goal.

A financial goal is not a strategy. I have heard leaders state that their strategy is to make money. While making money might be a measure of success, the way the organization goes about making money is the strategy. Even setting a specific financial goal does not provide sufficient insight into how to go about achieving it.

Accomplishing the key initiatives is not a strategy. Leaders often present complex charts and graphs describing multiple strategic initiatives aligned to core pillars and linked to performance measures. This impressive array of information is presented as evidence of their strategic plan. While key initiatives are important, they don't call out the game plan.

Beating the competition is not necessarily a good strategy. While in some cases competitive analysis is a viable approach for gaining market share, there are other ways to succeed. Leaders who focus excessively on the competition tend to neglect running their own organization.

A clear strategy statement sets strategic priorities that inform critical decisions. A successful strategy statement should make it easy for everyone to know what we as an organization will say yes or no to without much debate or confusion. The strategy statement defines the decision criteria for allocating the resources required to turn the strategy into action.

SETTING THE PRIORITIES

Priorities are decisions. Strategic planning is a conceptual exercise until the point of setting priorities. Once leadership sets priorities, they commit resources to set the strategy in motion. This is when leaders actually make the strategic decisions.

Because setting priorities is so important, it is helpful to express them as decision statements. Language becomes particularly important as leaders want to ensure that their priorities are correctly and consistently interpreted across the organization.

To eliminate misinterpretation as much as possible, it is advisable for leaders to write down the priorities as definitive statements. This exercise may require a few rounds of review to ensure the priorities are unambiguous. Consider the following examples for priorities set by a leadership team:

1. Expand regionally by opening new stores

2. Open five new stores in the Western United States

3. Open two company-owned stores in Los Angeles and San Francisco and three franchise-owned stores in Las Vegas, Portland, and Seattle

For the leaders who have been wrestling with the decision for months, the first statement seemed sufficiently clear. However, it failed to communicate essential information to others, who came back asking for clarification. Through back-and-forth communication, the leaders evolved their thinking to a more explicit statement that finally conveyed their priorities precisely.

Turning a strategic statement into a set of priorities helps an organization focus on what is most important. The priorities help launch the right initiatives and decommission projects that are not aligned.

How can you tell if your organization is focused on strategic priorities? To find out, ask a group of midlevel managers to describe what they see as the organization's top priorities. Their answers will provide a snapshot of what is currently consuming your resources.

If a representative group from your organization can consistently identify the top three to five strategic initiatives, they are highly focused, and it is very likely that the goals will be achieved. If you get a list of seven to ten important initiatives, the organization is not focused. You can anticipate that many initiatives will be left undone. If the list goes beyond ten, you can safely predict little to no progress on all fronts.

Time and again I leave a strategic planning retreat with a solid plan of action for a group of leaders to accomplish over the following twelve months. The plan is well laid out. The assignments are clear. But achieving the strategic goals depends on their ability to stay focused on a finite set of priorities through the weeks and months ahead.

* * *

"I will make a $70 million bet," Eric told me while planning the upcoming strategic planning event at his office. Eric was the CEO of a fast-growing technology firm. He knew he had only one shot over the next three years to make his strategy pay off. He also knew that he didn't know, at that time, which of the twelve or so key initiatives they were pursuing would prove to be most successful. Then, fixing his eyes on me, he said, "Your job is not to come up with the winning strategy but to help us follow a process that will deliver the winning strategy."

I was still processing what he meant. "I intend to put my bets on the table," he said to me while drawing circles on his glass board. "The investors expect us to use their $70 million investment intelligently. We don't know which bets will be the winning ones, no matter how invested we feel about some of our ideas. We need a process to help us define, concentrate on, and evaluate the most promising bets."

Eric went on to describe his strategic transformation process. From the strategic planning retreat, Eric expected to come out with twelve to fifteen key initiatives. But he was not intending to keep everyone working on all of them for long. The idea was to systematically pare them down by evaluating and eliminating initiatives every quarter based on evidence of success. Halfway through the year, he expected to concentrate on the six to seven most promising initiatives. By the end of the first year, he expected to be pursuing the three to five initiatives that were the most likely to succeed.

Eric realized that if they tried to pursue too many strategic priorities, nothing would be a priority. "When I was in college," Eric told me, "I was a professional juggler. I learned that just about everyone can easily keep tossing one ball up in the air without dropping it. With some training, most people can learn to juggle up to three items. It takes a lot of concentration, but it can be done. Professional jugglers can keep up to five items in the air at a time. That takes enormous concentration, but juggling professionals can do it. But when they add a sixth item, even professional jugglers can't keep any items up in the air. They all fall down."

The point was clear. Eric knew that too many initiatives would result in none of them getting done. Starting with too few would limit strategic options that needed to be tested and vetted. So, he intended to follow a process for systematically focusing the entire company on the strategic initiatives most likely to succeed.

I have shared this story about Eric with other clients, including his metaphor about trying to juggle too much. They readily agree with the point and are amused by the juggling story, but they seldom adopt the discipline to prioritize. I have noticed that even large corporations capable of deploying multiple teams and spreading their resources across multiple fronts still need to focus on a limited set of strategic priorities.

Executive teams determined to pursue ten or twenty strategic initiatives often fail within a year to accomplish any of them. Eric's company, year after year, whittled down an ambitious strategic agenda into the top three to five things that kept them growing at a 30 percent annual rate. It takes discipline and determination to focus, but focus is the key to a successful strategic transformation.

COMMUNICATING THE DIRECTION

Setting clear directions is one of the main functions of a leader. It is also one of the most prized responsibilities in any organization. Yet, it is seldom performed to the level required for everyone in the organization to clearly understand the direction.

Your strategies can only be accomplished when those who must execute them fully understand them. Each person in the organization needs to know the strategy and their role in accomplishing it. This is difficult, because there are various levels of specificity in direction setting.

Picture an inverted pyramid displaying the hierarchy of direction setting going from general at the top to specific at the bottom point. Sitting at the top is the vision statement, describing a direction in the most general way. At the bottom, there are specific success measures. Connecting these two ends, there are several elements, such as priorities, goals, objectives, initiatives, and deliverables that bring increasing clarity and definition to the direction.

HIERARCHY OF DIRECTIONS

GENERAL – CONCEPTUAL – LONG TERM

VISION
Guiding purpose

GOAL
Defined achievement

PRIORITIES
Allocation of resources

KEY INITIATIVES
Critical project

DELIVERABLES
Evidence of task completion

SUCCESS MEASURES
Indicator of achieved results

SPECIFIC – PRAGMATIC – SHORT TERM

Figure 4.2

The challenge for most leaders is to know exactly at what level to communicate the direction for the organization. Due to the nature of their role, leaders tend to be more familiar expressing directions in more general terms, describing the bigger picture. Unless such broad statements are followed up by additional specificity, however, the direction is too abstract to be meaningful to people at the middle or the lower levels of the organization.

Effective communication of the strategic plan starts with a compelling vision, followed by a set of strategic priorities, goals, objectives, and initiatives. In order to make the plan concrete and relevant to those who need to carry it out, they also need to know the actual deliverables and measures of success.

Conversely, there is a need for higher levels of participation, commitment, and ownership at the lower levels of the direction hierarchy. While it is expected of senior leadership to set high-level directions, it requires the involvement of those doing the work to define how it is to get done. People need to participate in defining the more specific elements of the strategic direction.

During strategic transformation, the Strategy Team is responsible for setting and communicating direction in terms of vision, priorities, goals, and objectives. The Activation Team plays a valuable role facilitating strategic alignment by involving groups in carrying out the initiatives, producing deliverables and reporting success measures.

The vision and strategic priorities help set meaningful goals, while the deliverables and success measures make the direction specific and relevant. When every person in the organization can explain the strategy in ways that are both meaningful and relevant to their role, there is clear alignment. When an organization achieves this level of alignment, they can accomplish extraordinary things in record time.

* * *

Julia showed up on-site unannounced. She asked to see how this heavy industrial manufacturing site had been doing with the sixteen operational improvements that had been required of them a year ago. If Julia had been just any customer, this surprise visit would still have been an uncomfortable experience. But in this case, she was representing their main customer, one of the largest oil and gas corporations in the world.

The site manager knew that about a year before, Julia had sent the company's executive team a clear message, possibly an ultimatum. In order to keep their business, each manufacturing site had to resolve gaps in product quality, safety, and reliability. After all, given that in their business industrial accidents could result in explosions, natural disasters, and human casualties, even small quality errors could be fatal.

Julia was making her way around the globe, visiting customer sites without advance notice. The point was to see firsthand how seriously her company's requests had been handled. She was used to seeing the pale faces of site managers unprepared to respond to her request. She had seen them scramble to bring up data showing some degree of improvement. She ultimately knew that, for the most part, these managers were putting on an act to save face, but in reality little had been done.

To her surprise, this plant was a different story. The plant manager seemed confident, even excited to show her their latest achievements. He called her into a meeting the next morning to hear a report from the sixteen strategic improvement teams that had been working on well-documented strategic initiatives. To her surprise, they were all prepared with current progress reports, charts, even photos showing before and after shots of what had been accomplished.

Obviously these teams had been working on the sixteen initiatives all through the year and were accustomed to reporting on progress. No one was caught unprepared. In fact, they took clear ownership for results of these projects. Most remarkable was that the team leaders were regular frontline employees who could articulate strategic goals and objectives with clarity.

In disbelief she asked to be taken to the manufacturing floor so she could talk directly with the rest of the employees. This would reveal if the improvements were real or the people at the meeting were simply doing a good reporting job. On the floor, she met with random employees, all of whom were well aware of the strategic goals and initiatives, as they had been participating as members of the sixteen teams. Evidently, the workers at this site had embraced quality, safety, and reliability.

To get official confirmation from her company's technical experts, Julia called for an international conference call with senior engineers the next day. They could test with rigor and discipline the quality of the work being done. On the other side of the call, frontline workers were answering with confidence piercing technical questions on the methodology and measurable evidence of improvement. By the end of the call, the gains were validated, and Julia requested that this approach be replicated at all other sites.

Behind the scenes, everyone at the plant knew that the approach Julia was requesting was critical to their success. The sixteen team leaders had been selected to form the Activation Team. Throughout the year, they met regularly to receive training and make improvements on the assigned strategic initiatives. Each team leader facilitated rapid improvement and gained confidence in their ability to make important things happen.

The site manager summed it up, saying, "In order to really improve, we needed to engage all of our employees to act as leaders, take initiative, and make improvements."

PRIORITIZING IN REAL TIME

Priorities are not fixed. They constantly change. So how we respond in the moment often determines our priorities. What we commit ourselves or others to doing is how priorities get negotiated in real time.

The Prioritizing in 4D framework, also known as the Eisenhower Matrix, is one of the best means of determining priorities in real time. This framework helps us determine the most appropriate response to an assignment, based on the importance and urgency of that assignment. The four approaches include deliver, decide, delegate, and delete. The following graphic illustrates these four approaches.

PRIORITIZING IN 4D

	Urgent	Not Urgent
Important	**DELIVER** Do it now.	**DECIDE** Schedule a time to do it.
Not Important	**DELEGATE** Find who can do it for you.	**DELETE** Eliminate it.

Figure 4.3

When a task is both important and urgent, the best response is to **deliver**. To do this we must:

- Confirm that the task is really important and urgent

- Explore fixed and flexible parameters

- Obtain a reciprocal commitment

- Set aside time and space for uninterrupted work

- Turn off distractions for a time

- Allocate time breaks for tasks such as checking and responding to emails

- Focus on delivering a completed task at a time

Sometimes a task is important but not urgent. In this situation, we need to **decide** when to do it. To do this we must:

- Validate the importance of the task

- Find possible times to complete the task

- Allocate sufficient resources

- Calendar events and participants

- Explain the importance of the task

- Store information for future reference

- Move back to deliver priorities

When a task is not important but is still urgent, the best response is to **delegate** it to the most appropriate person. To do this we must:

- Confirm the urgency level

- Find who is the best person for the job

- Explain the assignment and time frame

- Send an immediate status update

- Introduce who has been assigned

- Support the assigned person as needed

- Follow up to confirm successful delivery on the request

If a task is neither important nor urgent, we need to be empowered to **delete** it. Ironically, getting responsible people to recognize when they *don't* have to do something is the most difficult behavioral change to accomplish. For the organization, it is one of the most valuable things those people can do. To delete a task that is neither important nor urgent, we must:

- Renegotiate expectations

- Eliminate unnecessary work

- Reschedule meetings if not ready

- Postpone conversations that can wait

- Send an email instead of holding a meeting

- Meet for thirty minutes instead of one hour

- Remember that stopping is the most difficult part

To respond effectively to real-time situations, we need to ask effective questions to determine the relative importance and urgency of new requests. As we gain confidence doing this, we will know how best to respond. When responding, conversation cues help us learn how to say yes in a way that obtains a reciprocal commitment from the other person and to say no while offering realistic alternatives, so we're still providing value.

How people respond to reactionary work determines whether they will continue to do more and accomplish less or if they will work smart on the most critical tasks. Performance is the ability to accomplish those critical tasks and be able to say no to noncritical tasks. This enables people to say yes to critical tasks and perform as strategic transformation requires.

How to Say "Yes" to Obtain a Reciprocal Commitment	
• **Yes,**	1. Express an interest to the areas you are willing to commit.
• **If . . .**	2. Describe what you need from others in order to deliver on your commitment.
• **Then!**	3. Explain what you will do after receiving the contribution from others.

Figure 4.4

Every yes to a task should be accompanied by an "if ... then" statement. The employee demonstrates interest in the task but also immediately states what is required from others, what commitments are needed, in order to accomplish the task. Finally, the employee explains exactly what they can accomplish with those commitments from others. So this is not an unconditional yes, but one based on mutual commitments that will ensure that the task can and will be accomplished.

How to Say "No" and Still Be Valued	
• **Yes!**	1. Express full support for the areas you completely agree. Exclamation!
• **No.**	2. State what you cannot do at this time with current resources. Full Stop!
• **Yes?**	3. Propose alternative ways to still accomplish what was requested.

Figure 4.5

Many people are afraid to say no, because they fear they will be perceived as negative, as blocking progress. But being able to say no in the right way is essential to keeping control of work and making certain that the most important things get done. The first step is to say yes to the importance of the task, if it is indeed important. But then they need to say an unequivocal no if they cannot accomplish the task with their current workload and resources. Then they move back to yes by suggesting alternative ways that the task could be accomplished. With this approach, the person requesting that the task be done does not hear a flat-out no but an expression of interest (yes number 1) and recognition that there might be another way to accomplish the task (yes number 2).

The difference between successful people and really successful people, is that really successful people say no to almost everything.

—*Warren Buffett*

Which would you prefer, someone who always says yes but has trouble delivering, or someone who sometimes says no but always delivers when they say yes? If you need work on your car, which of the following two mechanics are you more likely to go to?

Jim is a friendly, positive guy who never says no. He's always ready to help you out and let you drop off your car. Unfortunately, because he never says no, he's always overbooked and rarely gets your repair done when he says he will.

Doug, on the other hand, is not quite so friendly—blunt is a good word for him. When you call, he'll ask you a few qualifying questions about the nature of the repair, and if he can't get your repair done when you want it, he'll tell you flat out. But if he tells you he *will* get it done when you want it, he *means* it—you'll get your car when you expect it.

When it comes to getting practical tasks done, most of us prefer to work with Dougs than with Jims. We trust the Dougs more, we rely on them more, because they are honest, straightforward, and get done what they say they will do. And that's the kind of people an organization will have if people feel empowered to say no when they have to, so they can say yes with confidence.

Prioritizing in 4D can help us quickly assess a new task and respond appropriately. These skills are valuable at a personal level and can also be applied to implement a prioritization process.

* * *

An IT department at a healthcare organization was overloaded with a growing list of high-priority technology projects. Requests came from various departments and influential individuals, each placing pressure on the IT department to deliver on technology solutions.

"We want to be seen as a responsive department, able to keep the organization on the leading edge through technology," the chief technology officer shared with me while at his office. "But we are now operating in a defensive mode, saying yes to too many things that we are not able to deliver, resulting in a bad reputation."

While trying to please everyone, working overtime and managing multiple concurrent projects, IT had unintentionally lost the trust of the organization. In working with them, I discovered that the IT department had over seventy active projects in its queue! This was an obvious target for improvement.

There was no way to properly assess the importance or urgency of any one project, as every project was a top priority to the requester. To solve this, we organized an IT steering team representing all key stakeholders in the organization. Their function was to evaluate and assign a priority to each project in the queue. The IT steering team met weekly and reported to the CTO.

Using the prioritizing in 4D approach, the IT steering team managed to delete some jobs, delegate others to contractors, place several projects on hold, and focus on only five projects at a time. This meant that the IT folks were never working on any more than five jobs at any given time. With this approach—and by learning how to prioritize and say no when necessary—the IT department became highly effective at delivering on promises and reestablished trust with the organization.

Putting your organization's house in order by intelligently prioritizing and empowering people to say and mean both yes and no will help you deliver on the strategic priorities. Staying focused is a key determinant of success.

NOTHING FAILS LIKE SUCCESS

The success achieved through focus can bring up so many opportunities that you could easily lose focus and ultimately fail. When faced with a prominent challenge, individuals and organizations naturally focus. However, after experiencing much success, it's very easy to get caught up in pursuing too many things at once. Individuals and organizations need to stay focused even as they become successful.

As the CEO of a large construction company, Scott had seen firsthand the effects of disciplined focus and the lack thereof. I was invited to speak at Scott's annual company meeting. While we were listening to the company's annual report, I noticed that under what seemed like unquestionable success, there were warning signs. Scott leaned over and whispered to me, "Nothing fails like success."

Scott had risen through the ranks by helping the company make bold moves that positioned it to grow during an industry downturn. The company was recognized as a state-focused player in residential home construction during the housing boom at the early part of the new century. They could hardly keep up with the demand, and they were making money at a rapid clip.

As Scott kept up with the market trends, he became increasingly uncomfortable with what he was seeing. He finally came to the conclusion that the highly profitable housing construction market was a bubble that was going to burst.

He shared this intuition with his executives and the board. He suggested that the company expand into different areas of construction. Many people in his company were incredulous, wondering why they would switch their focus from a booming market to something less certain. But Scott was persuasive, so they went along.

The company decided that if, in fact, the bubble burst, the government would be likely to step in to stimulate the economy and provide jobs. This meant that the company should start focusing on winning government building contracts. They figured that this would last a few years and then fall off, but by then the economy would be recovering and commercial construction would be hot, so they would switch their focus to commercial contracts. Eventually, the commercial market would cool down, too, and then they could circle back to the housing market once it had recovered.

Of course, their competitors thought they were crazy and were happy to snatch up all of the home construction business that Scott's company was leaving behind. But when the bubble did burst, the company was minimally exposed in the housing market, and they were ready to work on projects the government did indeed initiate to help the economy. Then, when the government contracts market was still healthy, they surprised their competitors once again by doing less of that business and turning to commercial building. When the government contracts dried up, again Scott's company was not overly exposed.

This strategy worked so well that the company became highly successful, while many competitors went out of business or struggled greatly. And that was when they lost their focus. They spread themselves out into multiple states and retained many of their markets, so they couldn't compete well in any one area. Projects started to go wrong. During the annual company meeting, they were facing these situations. And that's why Scott said, "Nothing fails like success."

Because, ultimately, it was their success that caused the lack of focus that ended their success.

At work and in life, we all need to get our priorities straight. To gain focus, we need to get clear about what matters most. To stay focused, we need to reduce or eliminate distractions and learn to prioritize in real time. In your drive for strategic transformation, you need to help others understand and act on priorities.

KEY TAKEAWAYS

- For your strategy to succeed, you need to increase your organization's focus on the most critical priorities by redirecting or eliminating less valued work.
- The most effective leaders stay focused on what matters most by working smart.
- To work smart, you need to regularly assess, adjust, and execute on the most critical priorities.
- A strategy is a game plan to achieve a goal by a set date.
- The strategy defines the decision criteria for allocating the resources required to turn the strategy into action.
- Once leadership sets priorities, they commit resources to set the strategy in motion.
- Because setting priorities is so important, it is helpful to express them as decision statements that can be accurately and consistently interpreted across the organization.
- Strategic plans could add a whole new set of priorities to people's already large workloads unless other initiatives get decommissioned.
- The prioritizing in 4D framework helps people determine the most appropriate approach to responding to an assignment, based on the importance and urgency of that assignment.

- The ability to know how to appropriately say "Yes" and "No" to assignments increases your value and influence in the organization.
- The success achieved through focus can bring up many new opportunities that could cause you to lose focus and ultimately fail.
- In order to succeed in your work and your life, it is important to be clear about your priorities.

CHAPTER FIVE

PEOPLE—DELEGATING RESPONSIBILITIES FOR RESULTS

L eaders bet their entire strategies on the people they appoint to carry them out.

Selecting the right people for the right jobs is one of the most important, and most difficult, decisions a leader has to make. Then, even with strong key players in place, leaders often fail to delegate responsibilities to those key players, hindering their ability to achieve results.

President Abraham Lincoln was familiar with this challenge. He had to execute a strategy on which hung the fate of the entire United States of America. And although he was the commander in chief during the Civil War, he had to rely on the commanding general he appointed to actually prosecute the war. On this decision alone depended thousands of lives.

Leaders bet their entire strategies on the people they appoint to carry them out.

Lincoln, an attorney and politician by trade, was not knowledgeable about the army at first. He had to rely on his own instincts and on the advice of others to make this appointment. He quickly learned that it was impossible to execute a winning strategy without having the right person to do it for you. He went through a number of commanding generals before he found the right one.

Lincoln first bet on Winfield Scott, the hero of the Mexican War. Back in 1847, Scott had been decisive and daring, but by the time of the Civil War, he was seventy-five, slower, less healthy, and far more cautious than he'd once been. Eventually, disillusioned by Scott's advice to yield both Forts Sumter and Pickens, Lincoln made a decisive move.

He brought in the young and highly popular General George McClellan to command the Army of the Potomac, though still leaving Scott as commanding general. McClellan feuded with Scott for months until the old man decided to retire and McClellan took over his position.

As commanding general, McClellan, who was a master at *preparing* troops for battle, proved to be highly reluctant to actually *send them into battle*—even when it was the obvious moment to strike. His excessive caution caused him to drag his feet on an intelligent plan Lincoln devised to bypass the twenty-five thousand Confederate troops in Manassas, Virginia, just twenty-five miles from the capital, and cut them off from nine thousand reinforcements waiting in Winchester, Virginia. McClellan's delay allowed the Confederates to reinforce Manassas, which led to the infamous Union defeat at Bull Run that put Washington, DC, itself in jeopardy.

McClellan continued to drag his feet on invading Virginia, despite the imminent danger to the nation's capital. Lincoln finally realized that McClellan was self-centered and bent on resisting his commander in chief at every turn. So he fired McClellan and replaced him with General Ambrose Burnside.

Burnside was known as a fighting general, but, unfortunately, as Doris Kearns Goodwin put it in *Team of Rivals*, "Though he was charismatic, honest, and industrious, he lacked the intelligence and confidence to lead a great army. He was said to possess 'ten times as much *heart* as he had *head*.'"[4] Within a few months, Burnside directed the army, against Lincoln's advice, to attack a heavily fortified Confederate position and lost thirteen thousand men—twice as many as General Robert E. Lee lost.

When Lincoln realized that Burnside didn't even have the confidence of his own military staff, he took over the duties of commanding general himself for a few months. When this proved impractical, he appointed General Henry Halleck commanding general.

But Halleck turned out to be a better administrator than a field general. Lincoln eventually came to think that he was "little more than a first-rate clerk," so the president had to do much of the strategizing himself.[5] Once again, he had the wrong man for the job. All

---

4   Goodwin, Doris Kearns. *Team of Rivals*. Simon & Schuster, October 2005.

5   Burlingame, Michael, and John R. Turner Ettlinger, ed. *Inside Lincoln's White House: The Complete Civil War Diary of John Hay*. Southern Illinois University Press, February 1999. 191-192.

along, painful defeats and stunning casualties piled up annually for the Union.

It wasn't until Lincoln heard about the exploits of General Ulysses S. Grant in the Western campaign that he found a commander he could trust to execute the war with an aggressiveness and strategic intelligence that matched Lee's. Grant was not an obvious choice—there were many questionable aspects about him—but he proved to be the right choice.

Grant took over as commanding general on March 10, 1864. His direct and ambitious drive delivered victories. In just a year, he engineered the defeat of the Confederate army, accepting Lee's surrender on April 9, 1865. The right man for the job was able to lead a swift and highly effective strategic transformation.

SELECTING THE RIGHT PERSON FOR THE RIGHT JOB

Knowing what to look for when selecting people for a position is the critical skill. The talent to spot talent is a valuable leadership quality, and one that leaders don't necessarily have. Fortunately, as with Lincoln, it can be developed, even if it requires some trial and error.

When selecting a key player in your organization, what do you look for? Competence? Integrity? Loyalty? Cultural fit? While these are the typical focus of selection interviews, they are poor predictors of future performance.

Competence is what most interviews try to assess. Can the person do the job? But competence alone is insufficient. Integrity is universally most cherished and yet it is difficult to assess properly. Loyalty is critical to ensuring that contributions will be aligned with a leader's goals. Without it the candidate quickly turns from an asset into a liability. But how can you assess loyalty? Cultural fit is how candidates get picked most frequently. Can the person work well with the rest of us? As much as we want to get along well with the new person, cultural fit is a lousy predictor of performance.

The best and most reliable predictor of future performance is past performance. Pay special attention to the trend of recent performance. A person's track record defines a path that, if properly mapped out, shows what that person is most likely to do next. To select the right person for the job, you need to know exactly what that person has been doing lately. Not what they *say* they've been doing, but what they've *actually done*.

The best and most reliable predictor of future performance is past performance.

Let's review a few examples of selection interview questions. All too often, selection interviews focus on competence, style, and fit by asking questions such as:

- What is your knowledge of (subject matter)?

- What is your management style?

- What did you like best about your last job?

- What type of company culture do you like?

After receiving an answer to the questions above, how likely are you to be able to predict future performance? Very unlikely! A more effective set of questions gets closer to understanding actual contributions. For example:

- What was your main contribution to the company in your last position?

- What did you do on a weekly and monthly basis in your position?

- What did you do in a situation when things did not work well?

- What did you accomplish within the first year on the job?

The time invested up front in a robust and rigorous selection process pays off over a prolonged period of time. Instead of just looking for competence, style, or cultural fit, you need to understand each candidate's work history—not just going over their résumé, but understanding *in depth* the role that this person played in each position and what exactly were their contributions.

The time invested up front in a robust and rigorous selection process pays off over a prolonged period of time.

By asking effective selection questions, you can gain a thorough understanding of someone's track record. While it may take time to conduct a thorough selection interview, it is far better than hiring the wrong person for the job. Too many leaders, and too many organizations, don't put enough thought into selecting the best people. They go with their gut instead of putting in the time and effort required to ensure that the people they hire have actually done what is required to excel in the position for which they're being hired.

Experience has shown me clearly the critical importance of making the right hiring decisions. For seven years, I worked with a hospital to help them select people for their executive level positions. The hospital was growing rapidly and needed to build a strong and united leadership team. For each top candidate, I spent three hours one on one, going over a set of assessment results. Over the years, I helped with dozens of executive hiring decisions for this hospital.

At one point, they asked me to interview a candidate for a chief financial officer position. The last CFO had left suddenly, and there was an urgent need to fill the role. A suitable candidate had made it to the final round, and the hospital seemed to view the last interview I did with him as a rubber stamp of final approval. They even wondered if I might expedite the process so they could extend an offer.

Knowing the importance of the position, I spent the full three hours interviewing this candidate, planning to report to the vice president of human resources immediately afterward. The offer letter was ready to be issued. During the course of the interview, I noticed that when the candidate talked about his prior financial work, he kept referring to "us" and "my team" instead of describing his personal accomplishments. "I want to know what specifically *you did*," I told him. His answers again drifted into team achievements.

"Are you going to give me a passing grade?" he asked jokingly at the conclusion of the interview. "You are a capable person," I said to him, "but I doubt you have actually been a CFO before." I said this point blank. He was shocked. I discerned from the interview that he had actually been a financial comptroller, but he had led others to believe that he had the experience of his supervisor, the actual CFO. Probably he felt that he was so well aligned with that

CFO, and had worked so closely with him, that he knew what the CFO's job was like and was describing his work as an extension of the CFO's.

Everyone in the hospital who had interviewed this man had come away believing he *had* been a hospital CFO! My in-depth questions about his past performance uncovered that he had never actually held the position—and the hospital was certainly not looking to train someone as a CFO on the job!

Maybe a three-hour interview sounds extreme to you, but having a third party interview your candidates in depth—without the pressure to fill a position and with the sole intent of truthfully scrutinizing every candidate to make sure they fit the profile for your positions—could save you a year or longer of having to live with the wrong hires. Put in that perspective, three hours isn't much time at all!

BUILDING A TALENT FACTORY

When you have a strong team of competent and united key players, people in the organization feel confident in their ability to execute a strategic plan. This confidence translates into positive morale, effective work, and tangible results. But getting there takes a lot of work. Most leaders have to build such a team and, once it's in place, cultivate a leadership culture within the team.

To develop a culture that supports strong and united leadership requires leaders to build a talent factory. A talent factory is an organization committed to developing people. People learn and grow—and the best of them thrive—in such an environment. Becoming a talent factory requires an investment in people, which, like every sound investment, is expected to deliver a substantial return. Leaders at a talent factory expect more of their people.

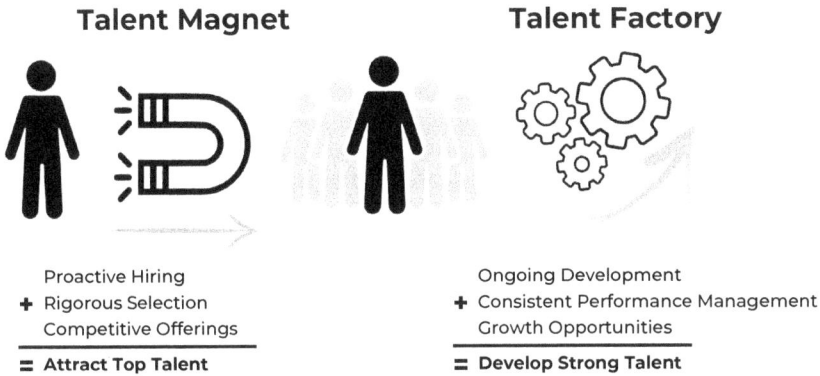

Talent Magnet

Proactive Hiring
+ Rigorous Selection
Competitive Offerings

= **Attract Top Talent**

Talent Factory

Ongoing Development
+ Consistent Performance Management
Growth Opportunities

= **Develop Strong Talent**

Figure 5.1

Constant learning. Regular feedback. Performance measures. Cross-training. Job rotations. Developmental goals. Stretch assignments. These are the typical elements present in a talent factory. It is not enough to just put in place random development programs. There needs to be a conscientious investment in people development, aligned with core values and consistent leadership practices, that matches your strategic goals.

There needs to be a conscientious investment in people development, aligned with core values and consistent leadership practices.

The opposite of a talent factory is a talent pool, a place where good people come, stick around, and stagnate. In such organizations, promotions are used as rewards for tenure, loyalty, or a good relationship with the boss. Talented people often don't find a way to advance there, so they move on—or worse, they quit working hard and stay! It's those who hang on that eventually rise to the higher positions.

To become a talent factory, you need to invest in people. Goldman Sachs, a company whose investments are known to beat market returns, is constantly investing in its people. Most Goldman Sachs traders start learning how to invest at the bottom, as floor traders. They are required to learn rigorous methods for managing risk and making sound investment decisions. As they progress, they are assigned mentors who help them gradually gain more independence with their trades as they increase their portfolio's value.

Even then, many traders make mistakes that lead them to be drawn out at some point in their tenure—meaning that their investment portfolio's value has shrunk to such an extent that it's closed down. At most companies, traders who get drawn out are fired. But at Goldman Sachs, they are allowed to invest with play money for a period of time, while they record what's happening to their investments over that period. Then they have to write an essay about what caused the failure of their real portfolio and what they have learned since from working on their practice portfolio. To be reactivated, these traders have to present the lessons they've learned to a group of senior traders, who judge if they are ready to return to the trading desk. This commitment to developing people is a major factor in Goldman Sachs's success. It is what it takes to become a talent factory.

While working with Fidelity Investments, I experienced what it's like being part of a talent factory. Fidelity constantly invests in people to develop a high level of professionalism and competence in their ranks. Many positions require employees to remain current, with advanced certifications in the financial services industry. Constant learning and formal training is part of everyone's job, which fosters a strong leadership culture.

At IBM, those who pursue a management track are required to experience various areas of the organization regularly, and deal with different kinds of challenges within each of these areas. By the time they become senior managers, they have a broad understanding of the company and the industry. While I was working at IBM, the company was going through a historic downturn. They were losing millions of dollars, but they continued to invest millions in leadership and training. I asked a high-level executive why IBM continued to put so much money into training when it was losing money. He told me IBM believed that it was through developing people that they would ultimately solve their problems and pull out of their financial difficulties.

Becoming a talent factory is a way of thinking seriously about your people. It is a strategic investment in becoming the best by working with the best. It is part of the employment value proposition. A year at a talent factory equals several years at an ordinary organization. The experience a person gains in such an organization makes them more valuable internally and to the broader market.

BECOMING A TALENT MAGNET

If a talent factory develops strong and united leaders, an organization that is trying to quickly build a strong team needs to become a talent magnet—a place where talented people really want to work. Even talent factory organizations need to attract top talent.

A talent magnet is an organization that creates a very attractive value proposition for the people it hires—it knows how to market itself to the most talented people. A talent magnet is always hiring, but always hiring selectively. They make it challenging to become part of the organization, so being hired by them is in itself an achievement.

Top management consulting firms are known to be highly selective, requiring candidates to go through a very rigorous set of interviews, including case analysis and recommendations. Candidates must record a video presenting themselves and discussing how to solve problems that are presented to them as a business case. These organizations are looking for individuals who can think critically, understand nuances and recommend reasonable solutions to real-life situations.

Talent magnet organizations create an allure to passing a challenging test and being selected to become part of the organization. Everyone in the industry wants to be selected, so there are usually many applying and few who get selected, which facilitates sorting through many qualified candidates to find the right hires.

A rigorous selection process is essential to becoming a talent magnet. If you only end up with one candidate for a position, that equals no candidates, because you have no choice. Only with several qualified candidates do you really have a choice—otherwise you're stuck with the default candidate.

Some companies use experiential test situations to reveal candidates' thinking and decision-making responses. I saw this firsthand as I was presenting a consulting proposal to a prospective client. This fast-growing company wanted to work with the very best. To screen talent, they created orchestrated situations surrounding the interview.

In my case, as I arrived at the front desk, I was told that the person who was supposed to interview me was running late. An assistant came to inform me about this and asked me what I wanted to do. I decided to wait a while. Later, the same person came again to say that the interviewer still hadn't arrived and asked if I wanted anything else. Noticing that we were losing the time for the meeting, I proposed that we reschedule. But when the assistant came back, she asked me to follow her to the conference room where everyone was waiting for me. This, of course, caused some stress, as I had about half the time originally allotted for the presentation.

A group of about seven people were sitting in the conference room ready for me to deliver my presentation. Then I found out that they had no cable to connect my laptop to the large screen. The group insisted that I do a brief verbal presentation, instead, without my slides. Once again, this added stress to the situation, but I did my best to condense a one-hour visual presentation into an engaging fifteen-minute verbal presentation.

When I finished, they explained that the entire situation had been a setup to test how I would react to the stress and challenges of the situation. The person who had come back and forth to tell me what was going on was not an assistant, but someone from HR who could observe my responses.

As they debriefed me on how I came across in the situation, I learned many valuable things about myself. They were really examining my demeanor—whether I was appropriately patient but also appropriately impatient. Whether I had a plan B for handling the situation and whether I really valued my time. Whether I could deliver a compelling message in fifteen minutes in my own words without visual aids. I received a lot of useful feedback on a situation in which I didn't even realize I was being tested! Fortunately, I was hired, although I received feedback on how to be more assertive about the value of my time.

A talent magnet is an organization that consistently attracts, selects, hires, and onboards the very best people. People talk about these organizations as the greatest places to work. But what makes an organization a great place to work?

Many organizations seek this appellation by offering attractive benefits and perks such as modern work areas, access to exercise facilities, a selection of healthy foods in the cafeteria, and playgrounds—not just for the employees' children, but also for employees to relieve stress.

Many of the best places to work do offer attractive perks, but rewards only work well when they support a strong work culture. To become a great place to work, a company needs to do more than just become a fun culture club. Strong leadership, employee development, respect for others, high engagement, and productive work practices are the foundation. It starts by helping people take responsibility for their work.

DELEGATING RESPONSIBILITIES

Assuming that a leader has enlisted strong key players, the *number-one* reason that strategic plans still fail to deliver results is that leaders tend to hold others accountable only for *doing* activities, not for *producing* results. This sets an expectation from the start that the strategic plan is just a set of initiatives to be carried out, actions to be taken, dedicated effort to be exerted. Everyone gets busy showing their commitment while entirely missing the point of delivering results.

The number-one reason that strategic plans fail to deliver results is that leaders tend to hold others accountable only for doing activities, not for producing results.

Lincoln's initial choices for commanding generals were good at doing what most commanding generals do, such as planning attacks, preparing the troops, organizing logistics, and building morale. They were fully accountable for all the right activities but completely failed at taking responsibility for winning battles—and the war. Grant's focus was to defeat the enemy, and everything else was in support of that goal.

Leaders usually expect others to take responsibility for their work, but too often this means holding them accountable only for their activities—not results. Holding people accountable (account-able) implies that they have to render an account of what they have done—their actions. This will inevitably undermine the results the leader hopes to achieve.

Making people responsible (response-able) means that they own an end result. They need to respond by making decisions and owning the consequences. When people take responsibility, the job is done only when the goal is achieved. Response-ability implies an ability to respond to situations without being conditioned by the environment. The criterion for success is simply achievement of a goal.

* * *

"We've got to fix the ER!" the chief physician officer almost shouted across the room while pounding his fist on a table. Everyone agreed. No one knew how to do it. The emergency room was constantly in crisis mode. Patients lined the hallways, people with injuries of all kinds and severities sat next to each other. Nurses bustled frantically around equipment, beds, and people. This was the daily routine for this rural area hospital ER—life's drama chaotically unfolding.

First management focused on improving the culture to increase collaboration between the doctors and nurses. It was obvious that, in such a high-stress environment, there was a need for better manners and emotional intelligence. The culture training helped. Morale increased for a while, but it was not enough.

Next management proposed workflow improvements. Implementing a more efficient triage approach helped alleviate the congestion in the hallways and expedite service. The improvements were more noticeable, but it was not enough.

Finally they decided to bring in a new leader from outside the hospital, who had run a best-in-class ER. The new ER director decided to set a simple goal, following a trend that was gaining momentum across many hospitals: posting their actual emergency room wait time on a billboard in a highly visible place—a real-time display of results.

Suddenly everyone in the ER had a very clear responsibility to deliver on a measurable result. Everything they were doing was measured by this single aspect of their emergency room service. Initially, wait times averaged thirty to forty-five minutes, which was quite embarrassing. But by improving every aspect of their service, they were able to reduce wait times to under ten minutes—and then the goal became to go for the recorded benchmark of under five minutes.

Their goal was to match their performance with the performance of the best ERs around the nation—and they were judged on a regular basis by everyone in the town on this result, because their wait time was posted beside the freeway for everyone to see! With this kind of motivation to achieve a very specific result—to become one of the most efficient ERs in the nation—they succeeded in dramatically improving service and reducing wait time in the ER.

All of their prior initiatives were just that—initiatives. Actions to be completed. But when the team became responsible for a clear, specific result and started working in concert toward that goal, the ER finally improved dramatically and permanently.

CLIMBING THE RESPONSIBILITY LADDER

The role of the leader in activating a strategy is to appoint the right people and not just make them accountable but also give them the responsibility to deliver specific results. Too many organizations don't set measurable goals or hold people responsible for achieving them —so their strategic transformations, their attempts to transform their organizations, aren't effective.

Too many organizations don't set measurable goals or hold people responsible for achieving them.

What is the difference between giving an assignment and assigning a responsibility? When delegating an assignment, you expect others to carry it out, to complete the task and report on progress against a course of action. When delegating a responsibility, you are interested in the outcomes, the impact of decisions and actions on the results. You may be interested in learning about the impact of specific actions on end results, but what a person is doing to achieve the goal is less relevant than achieving the goal.

As a manager, are you holding people accountable to complete assignments or are you making them responsible for delivering results? One way to tell how you are orienting your team to results is by paying attention to what is being reported back to you during meetings or via emails.

If your direct reports seem content to just report on the tasks they've completed, the effort they've put into a project, the amount of work that will be required to finish a job, then you are encouraging them, intentionally or not, to account for assignments, not to deliver results.

On the other hand, if your team reports on their performance relative to their goals, the impact of their actions on desired outcomes, identifying performance gaps, and proposing solutions to fill those gaps, you can conclude that you are requiring them to take responsibility for concrete goals.

It is one thing to be *given* a responsibility; it's quite another to actually *take on* that responsibility. The concept of a responsibility ladder shows how people can move up or down on the responsibility scale.

Going upward toward higher responsibility means that when you see something within your circle of influence that needs to be done, you own it as something you can help solve and ensure that it gets done properly. As you climb those rungs, you gain control of a situation and ultimately become more powerful.

Many people are good at pointing out problems and expecting others to solve them. Instead of being problem solvers, they are problem finders. They take satisfaction in noticing what's wrong and calling it out. Then they wait, hoping that someone will take care of it. They have reasons for not being the ones to act on it and blame others when no one steps up. But this approach leaves them feeling like victims of situations, powerless to act for themselves.

As a manager, what can you do to help people step up and take more responsibility? You can start by setting an example of what it means to be responsible. Make sure to demonstrate responsibility in the areas you are responsible for. But don't jump in and try to solve problems for others. This will only reinforce their hesitation to be more responsible. Make it clear that you expect them to solve the problems in their areas of responsibility.

Steps to higher responsibility:

- Explain the consequences of their actions.

- Ask them to regularly report on progress toward achieving their goals.

- Help them see and analyze the root causes for their results.

- Allow them to experience the consequences of their actions.

While this approach may seem to expose you, as the leader, to risks, it also puts the burden for dealing with such risks on the people to whom you delegate.

When appointing someone to lead a strategic initiative, a common mistake leaders make is to delegate the assignment without giving the assignee real responsibility for the goals of the initiative. To avoid making this mistake:

- Ensure that people understand the importance of the assignment.

- Have them participate in setting the goals.

- Support them in their decisions about how to deliver the desired outcomes.

- Have them report on their performance relative to the goals.

KEY TAKEAWAYS

- Leaders bet their entire strategies on the people they appoint to carry them out, so time invested up front in a rigorous selection process is critical.

- Instead of just looking for competence, style, or cultural fit, you need to understand each candidate's work history—understand in depth the role this person played in each position and what exactly were their contributions.

- A talent factory is an organization that cultivates people, mentors them through growth, and even helps them overcome failure—so the best can excel.

- A talent magnet is an organization that attracts the best candidates by making it challenging to become part of the organization, so being hired by them is in itself considered an achievement.

- Assuming that leaders have enlisted solid key players, the *number-one reason* that strategic plans still fail to deliver results is that leaders tend to hold others accountable only for *doing activities*, not for *producing results*.

- When you delegate a responsibility, ensure that the focus is on achieving the goal. While it may be interesting to learn about the impact of specific actions on end results, that is secondary to reporting on goal achievement.

CHAPTER SIX

STRUCTURE— DESIGNING ORGANIZATIONS FOR INNOVATION

Throughout the history of the world, every major innovation in technology, science, and society has been made possible by an innovation in human organization.

The role that organization played in the advancement of achievement throughout history is often ignored, or at least greatly underestimated. When thinking of innovations, we remember the Gregorian calendar, the printing press, the steam engine, the electric lightbulb, the computer, and, more recently, the internet. We admire the outcome, as if it just popped into life from the sheer genius of an inventor. Quietly hidden behind all these scientific advancements, humans have been figuring out how to do things differently—which has resulted in radically different outcomes. Every new level of achievement is made possible by an innovative organizational model.

Every new level of achievement is made possible by an innovative organizational model.

What is most important for strategic transformation leaders today is to recognize that we are living at a historical inflection point influenced by emerging organizational models. Leaders in government, business, and education can greatly benefit from taking advantage of this to create a significant competitive advantage.

Take two organizations doing essentially the same thing. Both offer similar products and services to the same market. Both have at their disposal vast financial resources, ample human capital, and access to advanced technology. Which one is most likely to prevail? History consistently shows that the one with the more advanced organization ultimately prevails, even if they initially have less talent or fewer resources.

Let's take a look at some examples from history, especially during times of war, as wars inevitably provide decisive winners and losers. The ancient Romans conquered their world through an organizational innovation. The Roman legion was the largest permanent military unit, comprising up to five thousand men who enlisted, trained, and operated as professionals with pay, rank, and retirement provisions. This gave the ancient Romans a superior advantage over informal tribal or city-state militias. The Roman Empire also provided a higher standard of living conditions for its citizens, making it convenient to become part of the empire.

From the seventh to tenth centuries, the rise of Muslim nations, springing from the Middle East and expanding into Europe, Africa, and Asia, revealed a new organizational model based on the Islamic ideal of society. Islam became a force for civilizing a world in turmoil, bringing a sense of purpose, law, and order.

During the European Renaissance, the resurgence of the arts and religious reformation was connected with the invention of the printing press.

But we often miss the fact that all these accomplishments were made possible by the expanding influence of kingdoms based on a legal feudal system. Gutenberg was able to pursue the printing press because he was sponsored by the king of Germany, who was seeking to break away from the influence of the Catholic pope by making the Bible available in the German language. Many other kings followed this model, opening up access to books and new information for their people.

In modern times, we recognize that American independence and creativity was driven by a representative form of government. This organizational innovation gave a decisive competitive advantage to George Washington and the colonists who fought during the American War of Independence, ultimately overpowering the British armed forces, which represented the older organizational model.

The industrial revolution is most known for the invention of machines and technology, but what is often overlooked is that corporate entities based on the bureaucratic model made such inventions possible. General Electric, Ford Motor Company, General Motors, and Westinghouse, to name just a few, became the economic titans that funded the inventors and spread their inventions worldwide.

Bureaucracies, now associated with everything that is deplorable, inefficient, slow, and cumbersome, were in their time an organizational innovation. As an innovative evolution to the hierarchy, the bureaucracy vested special and defined powers in an office, or bureau. The office, not the person in office, was endowed with authority, making it far more simple to move people around as they advanced in their careers or moved on to new opportunities. The word *management* has the Latin root *mano*, or *hand* in English, referring to the current handler of the office/bureau. Bureaucracy gave birth to modern management.

In recent decades, we have witnessed the rise of massive corporations based on this prevalent organizational model. And, yet, the most successful organizations of *our* times are moving away from bureaucracy, in search of faster, more responsive and innovative ways to get work done. Companies like Google, Facebook, and Apple downplay rigid management structures and formal roles and responsibilities in favor of collaboration, teamwork, and agile decision-making.

Not surprisingly, the companies that are building the internet, cloud services, and artificial intelligence operate more as human networks than as bureaucracies. In order to be able to create innovative technologies, they had to innovate their organizational frameworks. To deliver innovative solutions, organizations have to empower autonomous teams. Leadership is more based on influence and contribution than on position and management rank.

As has been the case with every organizational innovation, there is a countercurrent reacting against this change. We see today a shift toward the concentration of executive powers, in the forms of nationalism, authoritative systems, and even dictatorships. The resurgence of the authoritarian command-and-control models may seem to contradict movement toward more collaborative organizations. But such has been the case with every transition; there is always a seemingly more powerful opposing force defending the establishment against new models of organization.

Today, it is clear that the direction of progress points not to the models of the past but to the emerging models that drive economic growth and personal development. Strategic leaders can best position their organizations for growth in the new century by fostering a more collaborative, empowered, team-based organization. The greatest value being created today comes from innovation. It is almost a strategic imperative across industries. There are immediate and practical benefits to be gained by building an organization that facilitates innovation.

ORGANIZING FOR THE PEOPLE, BY THE PEOPLE

People and structure. Which one comes first?

Most scholars and consultants will authoritatively proclaim that structure should *not* be designed with particular people in mind. People may come and go, but the organization stays in place. The structure and roles define what competencies are needed. Then, you need to assess the people you have to see to what degree they meet the requirements. If there are gaps, they need to be filled by hiring the right people to fill them. There is no way to know up front who is best qualified for a job unless the job is first defined. All this makes a compelling case for defining the organization first and then deciding who fills which roles.

Most executives and entrepreneurs will readily admit that the key players have already been chosen, or at least are firmly in mind, when they create an organizational structure.

The case for designing the organization before committing to the individuals seems logical. The problem is that this is seldom the case in real life. Most often, the people are already in place and frequently sitting at the table designing the new organization. Most executives and entrepreneurs will readily admit that the key players have already been chosen, or at least are firmly in mind, when they create an organizational structure.

Yes there are empty boxes in the organizational chart to be filled and possibly entire new groups to be built from scratch. But managers know all too well that it is futile to attempt to define a group's structure in the absence of a group leader, because the leader will ultimately build the team. There is ample evidence pointing to the fact that people come first, at least the key players, before the organizational structure is defined.

As I write this section of the book, I'm experiencing this people–structure tension firsthand. I'm a subject-matter expert in a large government transformation. I work with senior government officers and senior consultants from the top firms around the world. Our task is to modernize a government agency, and a key deliverable is proposing a new organizational structure.

As consultants following a well-prescribed methodology, according to the scope of work in a contract, we dutifully conducted an assessment phase, followed by a strategy phase, which will result in an organizational structure. Then and only then will we proceed to define the roles and responsibilities required by the new organizational model. This rigorous methodology lends authoritative discipline and logic to our recommendations.

The deliverables are anxiously awaited as we complete each step of the process. The final organizational design is supercharged with high expectations, as is the final recommendation on the new government structure. The stakes are high for many people's careers, relationship networks, and professional aims. You could think of the consultants as physicians who work at the operating table to perform skillful surgery that will make the patient whole again.

Stop! Reality check.

While all this is true, every interaction we have, from the initial conversation with the project sponsor to the weekly meetings with client groups, is laden with subtle expectations, explicit requirements, and back-office negotiations to position specific individuals in key roles well ahead of any organizational design. In fact, the meetings that help create the new organization structure are *sponsored and attended* by those who will play the key roles in the emerging structure!

You might think that we are betraying our own methodology by operating this way. Much to the contrary, the only practical and functional methodology is to involve key people in the process of organizational design. Sorting leaders first, based on their professional aptitude and political acumen, allows for a realistic and implementable organizational design. Otherwise, recommendations are no more than words on paper.

Validating this point in his best seller *Good to Great*, Jim Collins concludes after ample objective research that the companies that made the leap from good to great put people first and strategy and organization second. Collins devotes an entire chapter of his book to making the point "First Who, Then What."

The Strategic Transformation Framework does put structure before people, as is widely accepted and expected, but I purposefully organized this book so that the chapter on people came before the chapter on organizational design. This is a deliberate mixing of the two approaches intended to portray the interrelationship between people and organization.

So, which one comes first? It depends! Most situations favor practice over theory, which results in designing the organization with specific people in mind. Yes, there will be empty boxes and question marks, but the organization will be populated as it is being designed.

ALIGNING THE ORGANIZATION TO THE STRATEGY

For centuries, the newspaper enjoyed a prominent and distinguished place in society as a symbol of information. With the advent of the internet, however, several newspapers started publishing online versions. In less than ten years, most readers switched their preference to receiving the news online. By the mid-2000s, the news media industry was experiencing massive disruption. Most newspapers went online, and access to the news became essentially free.

The entire industry was in search of a new business model. Selling advertisements didn't support their professional journalist operations. Selling subscription access to in-depth content attracted only a few customers. News media giants attempted to spawn innovative start-ups, but their prevailing corporate cultures would not support the pace and agility required to succeed.

In January 2008, the *Financial Times* decided to acquire Money-Media, seeking to gain a position in quality news and analysis for the global money management industry. Money-Media was a tech firm in the news industry. Focused on being the premier source of specialized intelligence for the sophisticated customer, Money-Media kept hundreds of thousands of readers current with must-have information in their respective fields.

Money-Media's culture was entirely different from the parent *Financial Times*. And while located only a few blocks away in midtown Manhattan, Money-Media operated as a dynamic and entrepreneurial tech start-up. The organization was flat. Teams operated as semi-autonomous pods. Everyone worked in open areas.

Given the need to deliver highly specialized and timely news to target audiences, Money-Media launched a series of subscription-based services, each operating as its own independent start-up team. This nimble structure gave the *Financial Times* and Money-Media a competitive approach to monetize content through a new business model.

* * *

The best and most efficient way to operationalize a strategy is through the organizational structure. The idea is to align the organization to key strategic objectives. The organizational design concentrates resources and empowers leaders to carry out strategic objectives.

The best and most efficient way to operationalize a strategy is through the organizational structure.

Let's say, for example, that, after significant consideration, a leadership team defines five strategic priorities, each described by a set of more specific strategic objectives. The leaders are willing to make a long-term commitment to the strategy. Their attention then turns to ensuring implementation of this strategy.

The best way to activate their strategy is to design an organization around the five strategic priorities, including building the capabilities that make it possible to deliver on the strategic priorities. Each strategic objective is best served when a leader is responsible for achieving that objective. Each leader receives resources proportional to the set of objectives assigned to their area. Each area acquires or develops the capabilities necessary to achieve their respective objectives.

Consider the effects of not doing this type of organizational alignment. What happens then? In the same theoretical case, after fully committing to the five strategic themes the leadership team continues to operate in their familiar functional model. The heads of research, engineering, production, sales, marketing, and customer service all vow to support the strategy by working collaboratively as a team.

As they return to their respective areas, the daily functional priorities begin to consume their attention. The people on their teams are more committed to their functional expertise than to any business goal. After all, their performance is judged by how well they do their part, as they are not responsible for any company goals. While leaders support the goals, their day-to-day decisions reflect greater commitment to their function.

A year goes by and the leadership team realizes that while everyone worked diligently all year long to advance the strategic goals, no one was ultimately accountable for any one of them. When everyone is accountable, no one is responsible.

As simple as it may sound, aligning the organization to the strategy is the most effective way to predict that the strategic objectives will be achieved. This kind of organization requires a significant commitment to the strategy, which makes the organization results driven.

Aligning the organization to the strategy is the most effective way to predict that the strategic objectives will be achieved.

Some organizations are intentionally operationally driven instead. They are less committed to a set of strategic goals than they are to their core capabilities. These organizations focus on optimizing what they do best. In such cases, it works best to focus on the operating model rather than the strategy.

DEFINING THE TARGET OPERATING MODEL

Form follows function. Every organization is perfectly designed to achieve the results it is currently producing. All too often, we continue to work under the existing structural forms and hope to deliver significantly better results. But when the organizational structure stands in the way of desired results, progress is slow or stagnant.

Operating models require an understanding of an organization's business. You need to ask, "What are we trying to create here?" This makes it easier to step outside the current structure. If you don't ask this question, you'll be stuck doing the same thing over and over again, what I call "re-creating a Chinatown."

When people migrated out of China to various parts of the world, they re-created a replica of a town in China wherever they landed. You can find one in most major cities. It was not necessary for these immigrants to do this, but their mindset was still so prevailingly Chinese that they couldn't think of anything to do but re-create a Chinese town in their new country.

Many times, organizational leaders display this Chinatown mentality. They've been thinking in hierarchical terms for so long that they can't get out of that mindset. They say they want to create a more innovative organization, but then they start worrying about who will be the vice presidents, who will be the directors, and so on, and they end up creating a "new" structure that looks much like the existing one.

As you describe what you really do as an organization, you start coming up with interactions and linkages that are necessary between you and your customers and between different groups within the organization.

One of the strengths of the strategic transformation approach is the ability to translate strategic priorities into operating models. As the leader aligns people and the organization with the desired results, progress happens faster and more predictably.

The challenge for most leaders is to know how to do this while operating in the existing organization. Before proceeding with a reorganization, it is helpful to define up front the desired operating model. An operating model is a conceptual framework describing how the work is ideally done. Free from the structures of an organizational chart, the operating model allows people to conceptualize a better way to get things done.

Operating models make direct links between strategic themes and the end-to-end process inside and outside the organization.

For example, a financial services firm recognized the strategic value of linking independent investors with investment technology platforms and expert financial advisors who can help them make sound choices. This resulted in customized buying journeys adapted to the unique needs of each customer. The emerging operating model required a shift to a customer-driven, service-oriented organization.

Another financial services firm recognized that their competitive advantage was in the depth of their investment expertise and their ability to give professional advice to high-net-worth individuals and funds. This realization helped them define an entirely different operating model. Their strategic priorities now emphasize customer relationships with, and developing industry expertise for, selective customers. This resulted in a partner-driven organization emphasizing assets under management and thought leadership.

Defining the end-to-end process helped these organizations conceptualize new operating models. How the organizational model facilitates or hinders such key interactions and linkages determines the level of the organization's alignment with the strategy. Using this type of analysis to determine the best organizational model is far more productive than starting with moving people around the boxes in an organizational chart.

DESIGNING THE ORGANIZATIONAL STRUCTURE

Structural design is one of the most powerful and lasting devices a leader can use to trigger change. Because of this, it needs to be used with caution and discretion. Organizational change is very disruptive, as it directly affects people's jobs and lives. Overusing reorganization as a tool for driving change leads to increased stress, lower morale, and a decrease in productivity. So, it is best to think through a reorganization carefully and implement it with minimum disruption.

Structural design is one of the most powerful and lasting devices a leader can use to trigger change.

When translating an operating model into an organizational structure, it is necessary to define what functions need to be prioritized. Some functions become more critical than others to the strategy. This often leads to prioritizing functions as being essential, strategic, supportive, and administrative. Notice, however, that labeling a function as being more important than another carries huge negative implications for the people working in that function. It is important to recognize that all functions are needed and valued for their contribution, regardless of their prioritization.

To build an organizational structure, it is useful to recognize the various organizational design options available. Different organizational structures provide unique advantages in governance, decision authority, span of control, checks and balances, degrees of specialization, and information flow. Some of the most common organizational structures are:

Organizational Structures

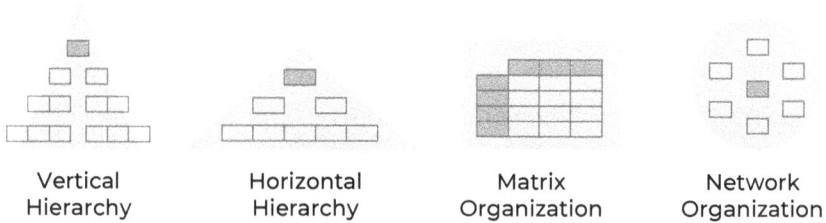

| Vertical Hierarchy | Horizontal Hierarchy | Matrix Organization | Network Organization |

Figure 6.1

VERTICAL HIERARCHY

The vertical hierarchical model is the most popular organizational structure for maximizing control and alignment. It works best in stable and predictable environments where there is a need for centralized decision-making and direct control over execution at each level.

HORIZONTAL HIERARCHY

The horizontal hierarchy pushes decision-making to the lower ranks, relying on the knowledge of the people doing the work to decide how it needs to be done. The role of the leaders focuses more on the management of resources, setting general guidelines, and reporting progress across multiple fronts.

MATRIX ORGANIZATION

The matrix structure aligns people's roles to multiple leaders, where the functional leader usually controls resources, and there are secondary layers of alignment to product, market, or regions. Matrix organizations can deliver complex solutions through cross-disciplinary interaction, yet they require significant coordination.

NETWORK ORGANIZATION

Network organizations are highly responsive to change, agile, and innovative. They achieve this by empowering individuals to form task forces, project teams, or communities of practice to tackle time-sensitive priorities. This requires teams to form quickly, collaborate intensively for a time, then disband once the task is accomplished.

Agile practices support network structures and provide the tools for iterative, dynamic execution of a transformation. Network organizations, however, are quite complex and difficult to manage. Leaders guide through vision, culture, and incremental wins.

Complex organizations often operate a combination of structures in different areas or even overlapping in some areas. In order to function in a complex organization, it is critical to review on a regular basis who does what.

UNDERSTANDING WHO DOES WHAT

Excitement was high at the Compass Fair. Employees from every department had been preparing for weeks to explain their function in simple terms to the rest of the organization. The Compass Fair gave everyone the opportunity to describe their roles and responsibilities and learn what others were doing. In one afternoon, employees from all locations came to a central place to meet, interact, and learn from each other.

"It was one of the most productive work activities we've had since I've been here," commented an associate with over seven years at the company. "I finally learned what everyone does around here and how my work fits into the bigger picture."

Said another, "It was great to bring everyone into one area and be able to meet them at a personal and professional level."

Like most large and well-established modern corporations, this organization operates a complex, multilayered matrix organization. Associates need to coordinate work across several teams and functions. Teams are constantly required to check with other teams in order to deliver customer solutions. The need to understand who does what is a constant requirement.

After several rounds of defining the ever-evolving organizational structure, operating model, end-to-end processes, and RACI (responsible, accountable, consulted, and informed) matrixes, there was a need to just get everyone together to fully understand how it all worked. The idea of the Compass Fair was for everyone to learn the model by having to teach it to others.

Over twenty stations represented each of the teams in the organization. Groups prepared ten-minute presentations describing their functional areas, which were followed by ten-minute question-and-answer sessions. Two or three designated presenters from an area addressed roaming groups of ten to fifteen associates every twenty minutes. The assigned presenters were released from their station after an hour so they too could join a group to learn from other stations.

The roaming groups were intentionally organized to include cross-functional associates. They were asked to visit each station, learn what the group at the station did and then answer a set of test questions in a mobile app. The results of their answers were scored and displayed as part of a fun contest with awards such as a paid day off work. The knowledge mastery contest incentivized individuals and teams to learn as much as possible about each function.

A Compass Fair-like event, besides being a highly engaging company activity, is valuable as a way to synchronize intelligent collaboration across a large number of people who worked interdependently. It is a way for people to learn the roles and responsibilities of others, and by doing so better understand their own roles and responsibilities. And when they know better, they can do better.

Nine months after the Compass Fair, this organization reported over one hundred big wins and success stories. Some of the wins highlighted operational improvements, others better working relationships. And, in some cases, they showed measurable gains through significant impact on how the organization operated. What was true for individuals was true for the organization—once they knew better, they were able to do better.

KEY TAKEAWAYS

- History consistently shows that the organization with the more advanced organizational structure ultimately prevails, even if it initially has less talent or resources.
- Most scholars and consultants will authoritatively proclaim that an organizational structure should not be designed with particular people in mind—but in real life there are almost always people in place or in mind who must be taken into account when the organization is designed.
- The best and most efficient way to operationalize a strategy is to align the organizational structure to your key strategic objectives.
- Operating models/frameworks require an understanding of your organization's true business/operational model—you need to ask, "What are we trying to create here?"
- When individuals within an organization know better what everyone else in the organization is doing, they—and the organization—do better.

CHAPTER SEVEN

PROCESS— STREAMLINING WORKFLOW TO DELIVER OPERATIONAL GAINS

Everything in life is a process.

Most of the time, we work *inside* our process, missing the greater opportunities that working *on* the process could deliver. There are effective ways to simplify and streamline your process, eliminating busy work in order to focus on work of higher value.

Think about the process of your life as a series of subprocesses operating at various levels interdependently. Within the larger process of your life cycle, these subprocesses include things such as relationships and family, work and career, health and fitness, and many more. You do your best to fit elements of each subprocess into a daily routine, creating an overall daily process.

When a day goes well, you feel good, because your daily subprocess worked out as intended. When it doesn't feel good, you try to make adjustments so things run smoother the next day. You feel a degree of success when you experience consistently predictable outputs from a particular subprocess. Yet you seldom pause to analyze that subprocess. We tend to work within our existing process and seldom take the time to review the process itself, missing out on the prospect of finding more productive ways of doing things.

A critical competency for the strategic transformation leader is to deliver operational effectiveness by streamlining the core workflows, the subprocesses, in an organization. This starts by being able to see the core subprocesses of an organization and conceptualize better approaches to them. Being too familiar with the core subprocesses may keep some leaders from seeing the bigger picture—the macro process of the whole organization.

The macro process is essentially the business model describing how the organization interacts with customers, shareholders and the workforce to turn inputs into higher value outputs. When a macro process works well, inputs of relatively low value consistently produce outputs of significantly higher value.

Take, for example, the stereotypical high-tech start-up. A group of three to five techno-entrepreneurs, cranking code on their laptops with nothing more than their smarts and imagination, come up with a new application within a few months that gets used by thousands of people and is soon valued at millions of dollars.

The macro process that makes this modern miracle possible is the effective interaction of systems architects, software developers, target customers, marketing geniuses, sales pros, and venture capitalists. Aligning all these components in the right steps and sequence turns ideas into fortunes—a highly effective macro process!

Compare that with the notoriously inefficient healthcare delivery process. We are trying to create a process for something quite common, people getting sick and needing care. The existing solutions are extremely complex, expensive, and somewhat inefficient. The macro process involves doctors, nurses, hospitals, medications, pharmaceutical companies, insurance providers, and government regulators. The process is costly and challenging for everyone involved. No wonder that customers are called patients—they need ample amounts of patience to navigate the system.

There are valuable opportunities at hand for those who can conceptualize and bring to market a better way to offer healthcare. Creative applications of health sciences and alternative ways to offer preventative healthcare are beginning to redefine the landscape by offering entirely new models. Perhaps, one day, there will be an entirely new macro process for delivering healthcare.

What about your industry? Can you describe its macro process? And, if so, can you identify ways to exploit its inefficiencies or envision a simpler and better approach? If you can do that, you are ready to capitalize on major process-changing opportunities.

You don't have to redefine an entire industry to deliver substantial operational gains. Most repeatable operations become processes by design or default. When recurring work evolves into a process without proper design, there is usually room for process improvement. The first step is to identify the process opportunity. The next step is to target operational improvements to that process. In the end, if enough subprocesses get improved, it *can* change the nature of a company's macro process.

* * *

Four rows of blue-collar workers sat on their chairs as I walked into the training room. Arms folded. Grease on their clothes. Safety glasses still on. Two-way radios also on, just in case. Some had long beards, some had tattoos, and all were noticing that I did not look like one of them, even though I'd dressed down in a pair of jeans and a blue shirt.

Roll call. All sixteen present. Training, you could tell, was not their favorite activity—especially when their expected work output was not reduced during the time they spent in training. This collection of characters had been picked by management to lead the transformation of the manufacturing plant. Heath, the program leader, kicked off the meeting—and what became a transformational journey.

These change champions, as they were called, consisted of machine operators, shipping and receiving workers, floor managers, and some engineers. They were all highly skeptical that any good would come out of this training. The plant had taken many hits lately. Revenues were trending down, production was lagging, and morale was low. And they were not thrilled about putting in extra time for no apparent value.

But over the following nine months, the change champions truly changed both themselves and the company as they became engaged in process improvements. Each of the change champions was assigned a strategic initiative, the same sixteen initiatives mentioned in the manufacturing plan story in chapter 4. This is the behind-the-scenes story of how that amazing change actually happened.

We met regularly as a group for two hours. The first hour was spent learning about manufacturing process improvements and change management. The second hour was used to apply what they learned to their respective initiatives. Heath knew how to engage the change champions with meaningful and challenging assignments—dealing with the problems they had complained about and now had a real opportunity to help fix. Heath acted as their coach, motivator, and instructor and was the liaison with management.

As they got into the nuts and bolts of work process in a way they never had before, they became excited about making a difference. What excited them most was seeing improvements in the way the company operated.

Take the assembly workers, for example. This group assembled electronic components that regulated valves—a key component in what the company produced that strongly affected the overall quality of their products. The manager of this group told us that his area had already been optimized and there was no need for more improvement. He showed us production charts to prove his point as he explained that he didn't want to take people off the line to put time into this activity.

So we came back with a counterproposal. We offered to sponsor a free pizza working lunch with his group to get their input on ways to improve their work process. The employees were as skeptical as their manager at first, but gradually they all became engaged in this exploration and ultimately came up with *twelve ideas* to improve their optimal process. And when they implemented just the top five of these ideas, they *tripled* their output *and* improved the quality of the components they produced—all within just a few months!

Shipping and receiving was equally convinced that they were doing things as effectively as possible. But they, too, eventually committed to, and got excited about, improving their processes. After implementing various changes in their process, their on-time delivery significantly improved—up from their initial 75 percent—and after just a few months they were able to hit *98 percent* consistently.

In like manner, the stocking department improved their tracking of inventory using floor layout redesign and color coding and electronic tracking systems, which ultimately delivered large gains in inventory.

The entire operation became a model plant for the rest of their global corporation. The change champions were proud that they had made an impact on their company's bottom line to the tune of millions of dollars. Some of them stayed with the company with renewed interest, others moved up, and some went on to start their own businesses.

TARGETING OPERATIONAL IMPROVEMENTS

Everything we do in a recurring way can be defined as a process. How can you tell if the current process is working well, needs improvement, or needs to be entirely redesigned? If you know what clues to look for, you can assess an existing process to see if it's effective.

When a process works well, the work flows from inputs to outputs consistently. The start and end points are well defined. The steps between are repeatable. The outputs are predictable. And there is a process owner monitoring the process with performance metrics.

The following are signs that a process is working well:

1. Clear start and end points

There is a clear point of entry and final delivery.

2. Defined steps

The work follows steps that are defined in standard operating procedures.

3. Predictable outputs

The process delivers consistent results that can be predicted based on the inputs.

4. Process owner

There is someone assigned to oversee and monitor the process.

5. Performance measures

There are measures that track the process performance at different steps.

If you are experiencing recurring errors, predictable delays, bottlenecks, or capacity constraints, it is very likely that the process is broken. There are clear signs when you are working with a broken process.

If you are experiencing recurring errors, predictable delays, bottlenecks, or capacity constraints, it is very likely that the process is broken.

The following are ten ways to tell when a process needs improvement:

1. Errors: Recurring errors regardless of who is doing the job

2. Delays: Frequent delays regardless of the original schedule

3. Missed deadlines: Work usually takes longer than expected

4. Waste: Consistent waste of resources

5. Over budget: Work goes over the budget most of the time

6. Redundancies: Frequent duplication of effort

7. Disconnects: Unclear expectations between groups

8. Bottlenecks: Work piles up in one area while there's too little in other areas

9. Variance: Quality and quantity of output is not predictable

10. Process owner: It is not clear who is in charge of the process

If you notice any of these signs, you have an opportunity. A cumbersome or broken process is like driving a car on a highway under construction with frequent lane merges, detours, and closed sections. No matter how good your car is, the road conditions determine your speed. Conversely, an efficient process is like driving on a superhighway—the path is clear, smooth, and swift.

Before jumping into improving a process, you need to question the process itself. Should the workflow be improved, disrupted, or eliminated? Too many process improvement efforts focus so much on gaining efficiencies that they don't challenge the basic assumptions behind what's being done. Reassessing the value of what's being done may lead to greater improvements. This requires us to step back, look at the big picture, and identify what the customer really values about what we do.

When there are diminishing returns for increasing efforts, it may be a sign that the process is becoming obsolete. In this situation, individuals feel that their work is becoming commoditized. The function is considered necessary, but of less value relative to other functions.

The following signs point to a need to disrupt the existing process:

1. Decreasing need for the current outputs

2. Commoditization of the activity

3. Lower priority of the function

4. Other things are needed instead

5. There must be a better way of doing the task

If we conclude that a process needs to be improved or redesigned, there is a way to systematically analyze, design, deploy, and refine workflow to achieve optimal results.

ACHIEVING OPERATIONAL GAINS

The aim of process improvement or redesign is to deliver consistent outcomes of higher quality faster and at lower cost. To achieve these gains, academics and consultants have created several comprehensive methodologies. You may have heard of methodologies such as Six Sigma, Lean Management, Total Quality, Just-in-Time, Kaizen, Hoshin Planning, PDCA, or DMAIC.

The aim of process improvement or redesign is to deliver consistent outcomes of higher quality faster and at lower cost.

This section distills the extensive bodies of knowledge, tools, and practices from these methodologies into simple and practical approaches for achieving operational gains. The strategic transformation leader is advised to rely on an expert for advanced process improvement capabilities, if necessary, but these basic components will help you understand how to lead such initiatives in a direct and practical way.

The five steps for process improvement are:

1. Assess the current process.

2. Map the current process *as is*.

3. Create the process as it *should be*.

4. Roll out the new process.

5. Continue to improve the process.

A high variance that swings unpredictably means that the process is out of control. When a process is out of control, you can assume opportunities for incremental improvements that bring the process into a controllable state. If the variance is relatively small and predictable, it means that the process is in control. When a process is in control, you can assume it is optimized and any improvement will require an entirely new process design.

After you have this information, estimate the ideal output when everything is working optimally. The ideal output is essentially a process improvement goal based on what is theoretically possible. If every step were to be optimized, you may ask what the ideal output level is.

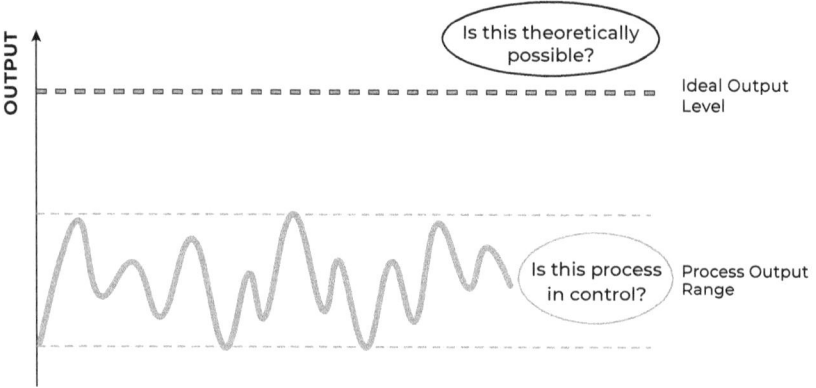

Figure 7.1

*If I had six hours to chop down a tree, I'd spend
the first four of them sharpening my axe.*

—*Abraham Lincoln*

Process improvement requires mapping the current process as is and then defining a streamlined process as it should be. If no formal process exists, there is no "is." Most often, however, there is a process, even if it has not been planned or formally documented.

To define the current process, capture the way the work is getting done at the current time. The process scope is defined by the start and end points of the process, usually referred to as the inputs and outputs. It is advisable to start defining the outputs, then the inputs, then finally mapping the steps between the two end points. Project constraints are the guardrails within which the process functions, and may include elements such as existing resources, quality standards, or legal regulations.

To map the process, write the steps in sequential order, assigning each step to a person or a group. Documenting the process as is helps everyone understand who is doing what and in what order. After completing the as-is process map, analyze the obvious process inefficiencies, redundancies, or disconnects. Identify the areas that cause the most problems.

While it is important to document the process *as is*, that activity should not consume more time than it deserves. Plan to save most of your time to create the process that *should be*. Creating a better process starts by estimating the ideal output. Setting the ideal output as a target gives a measurable goal to aim for, even if it is not initially considered realistic. This helps people think creatively about ways to imagine a better process.

Creating how the process *should be* begins by fostering a creative environment, where people feel free to brainstorm. To ensure a breakthrough, you may even have breakout groups work in parallel to engage in a process design competition. Typically, the group ends up adopting the best ideas from the different breakout groups to build the best possible process.

As you map the should-be process, document the steps in sequential order. This is not a time to clarify all the implications of each step. Instead, keep asking for a more efficient way of doing things, challenging the group to push the limits.

After achieving a draft of the new process, leaders need to approve it. Then it is advisable to test the process. Initially it can be tested conceptually. Eventually a pilot test is advisable before going live. Testing the process usually results in further adjustments to the initial design. When the process passes the tests, it is time to roll it out in the real world.

OPTIMIZING THE OPERATIONS

An effective process rollout ensures ease of adoption of the new process and the best chance to achieve the maximum level of success. Having involved all the process stakeholders in the design phase helps increase the chances of a smooth adoption during the rollout.

Following are the advantages and disadvantages of three different approaches to rolling out a new process:

PILOT TEST

1. There are high risks if the new process fails or disrupts work.

2. The new process may still have bugs that need to be worked out before full implementation.

3. There is high exposure if problems occur during implementation.

4. There is time to clean up the process before it is in full use.

HARD CUTOVER

1. There is high confidence that the changes will immediately improve the current situation.

2. There is strong leadership support for implementing the new process.

3. There is strong demand for the changes by users.

4. There are ways to clean up bugs in real time without significant consequences.

BY PHASES

1. There are multiple groups with varying degrees of readiness.

2. There is a need to gain the support of key groups before proceeding with full implementation.

3. There are mixed levels of leadership support for implementation.

4. It is possible to adjust the process as it is implemented.

To ensure that the new process is better than the previous one, you must measure the process outputs, analyze the results, and make additional improvements. This process of ongoing improvement can ultimately yield even more gains than the original design.

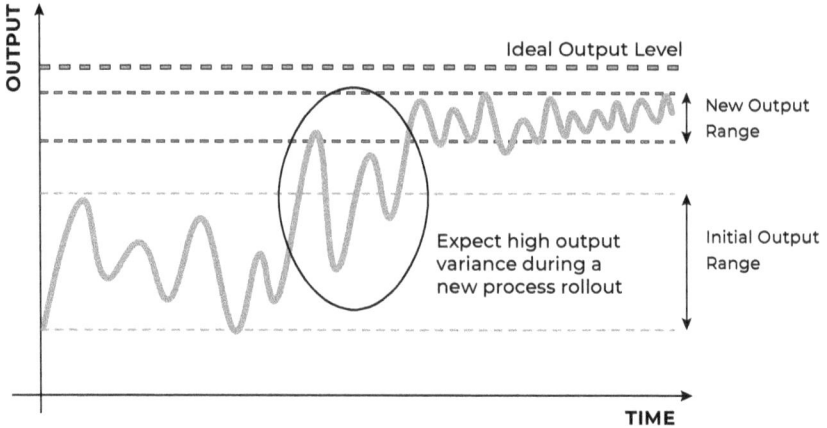

Figure 7.2

An attitude of continuous improvement recognizes that the process design will not be exactly right on the first attempt but only after making refinements. Continuous improvement accounts for the greatest gains as the process is optimized based on feedback. Effective and efficient processes lead to powerful and sustainable improvements.

The impact of a process that really works is huge and sustainable.

Effective and efficient processes lead to powerful and sustainable improvements.

PROCESS DETERIORATION LOSSES

Once a process is in place, one expects it to deliver target outputs consistently over time. This is usually the case during an initial period, when everyone is well trained and fully compliant. Unless the process is actively managed, however, outputs tend to decrease over time. Standards may become lax and new hires may deviate from the procedures, resulting in as much as a 20 percent performance decrease over time.

To counter this downward trend, practice continuous process improvement, which leads to performance optimization. Process optimization may account for additional productivity gains of 10 percent or even 20 percent over the initial improvement. This requires actively monitoring the process, doing ongoing training, and regularly reviewing process standards.

As technology evolves, parts of the process could become automated. Using technology for process automation further reduces human error, lowers operating costs, and removes low-value-added manual labor.

PRACTICING KAIZEN

Kaizen is the practice of continuous improvement. *Kai* means change; *zen* means good. Kaizen means a change for the better.

> *That which we persist in doing becomes easier to do,*
> *not that the nature of the thing has changed*
> *but that our power to do has increased.*
>
> —*Ralph Waldo Emerson*

* * *

Japan was devastated after World War II. All the large cities but Kyoto were severely damaged. Industries were forced to shut down and lay off their workers. Roads were ruined, causing severe food shortages. Little hope was left for the country that once believed itself fated to rule the world.

As part of the reconstruction effort, the United States sent production experts to teach the Japanese how to rebuild their fledgling economy. Some of the US professors taught the Japanese managers production processes relying on statistical control methods then familiar to the US War Department.

Japanese workers learned continuous improvement, a concept that resonated with the Buddhist philosophy of kaizen. The concept is rooted in the ancient teachings of Buddha. It describes an ongoing process for making steady, incremental improvements.

Japan rebuilt its industry and rose from poverty to become one of the strongest economies in the world. This growth resulted in a quick rise in Japanese living standards, a more democratic society, and increased political stability.

The Japanese applied process improvement to many aspects of their manufacturing and management processes. Toyota, for example, developed the Total Quality System for all of its production processes, including its suppliers and distributors.

When the first Japanese cars entered the US market, Detroit car makers did not take them seriously. The Japanese were unfamiliar with US roads and driving conditions, so their cars were associated with small, low-cost, low-quality vehicles. Relying on process improvement techniques, however, the Japanese gradually improved their cars. Within decades, Japanese cars were far superior to any car being produced in the US.

The kaizen approach has been associated with the impressive quality of Japanese manufacturing, so it is used for improving production quality and increasing efficiency by companies all over the world. The outcomes of their process improvements benefit the living standards of many societies.

* * *

Processes may not be the sexiest subject, but having the right processes in place is essential to leading a successful strategic transformation. For this reason, a strategic transformation leader must take process seriously and make sure that more effective and efficient processes are put in place. Well-thought-out processes are the backbone of a strategic transformation, and a weak backbone can cause the transformation to collapse.

But processes, once in place, should not remain fixed. Rigid approaches that leave no room for adaptation and evolution soon become counterproductive. In today's rapidly evolving work environment, processes must be agile enough to take advantage of changes in market trends, client needs, and organizational changes. In the next chapter, we'll discuss how agile practices make this possible and speed up the transformation.

KEY TAKEAWAYS

- Most of the time we work inside a process, missing the greater opportunities of improving the process itself.
- Ten ways to tell when a process needs improvement are recurring errors, delays, missed deadlines, waste, going over budget, redundancies, disconnects, bottlenecks, variances, and no clear process owner.
- It's time to disrupt an obsolete process when you see a decreasing need for the current outputs, commoditization of the activity, lower priority of the function, other things being needed instead, and thinking there must be a better way of doing the task.

- You need to map your current process *as is* and then map it as it *should be*—asking your organization for more efficient ways of doing everything and challenging people to push the limits.

- You need to roll out the new process in such a way that it can be tested and improved before it is rolled out to the entire organization.

- To counter the inevitable gradual reduction of effectiveness with a new process, use continuous process improvement—kaizen—to achieve performance optimization.

CHAPTER EIGHT

AGILITY— ACCELERATING THE PACE OF TRANSFORMATION

Practice makes perfect. And agile practices make near-perfect possible faster. As a leader, you can accelerate strategic transformation by adopting agile practices. The agile mindset approaches end goals incrementally through design, deploy, test, and learn cycles.

Once you have the right people in place and establish the right organizational structure with efficient work processes, the next step is to adopt effective practices. This step gets us into behavior and culture through work habits that speed up the execution of a transformation. Adopting the right practices, behavior, and ways of doing things is the next step toward a successful strategic transformation.

The agile mindset approaches end goals incrementally through design, deploy, test, and learn cycles.

* * *

In the early days of search engines, the algorithms that were used to search for information were in their infancy. Many different platforms such as Yahoo!, Explorer, and eventually Google were competing to build the most effective algorithms. Software engineers and data analysts worked diligently to figure out the best ways to find what was on the internet and match it to what was on the end user's mind when searching.

Yahoo! started first and made one of the biggest contributions to searching by organizing the largest directory service, a collection of authoritative sites used for search results. But while Yahoo! still is one of the most recognized search engines, Google now commands about 70 percent of the search engine market.

Many factors can be associated with Google's preeminence over the competition. At least in part, it can be attributed to their early adoption of agile practices. From the beginning, Google constantly tested, developed, and released to market improved search algorithms that, while not perfect, were the best iteration at the moment. As a result of this continuous release approach, the Google search engine was—and is—constantly evolving.

In the early days of search platforms, most companies followed the traditional approach to designing, developing, testing, and releasing search code. They worked on their algorithms, tested and fine-tuned them, and only when they felt those algorithms were ready for market did they deploy them. It took weeks, sometimes months, before they would be ready to release a new version of their search engine. In the meantime, Google's continuous release approach allowed them to constantly analyze, develop, and redeploy code *in real time*. Most users came to accept that Google's search engine was constantly in flux and that this delivered incrementally better search results for them.

* * *

Successful strategic transformation builds and sustains momentum. If execution takes too long without demonstrating material results, people start questioning the value of the strategy. Commitment begins to dwindle and doubts rise. Agile practices solve this by delivering regular wins that prove the viability of the strategy. Regular short-term wins provide the promise of long-term success critical to building and sustaining momentum during execution.

A long-term approach to delivering results is no longer acceptable—or effective. We've all been part of projects where the organization was told, "Don't expect to see any results for the next year. And culture change takes at least two or three years. This requires a big investment on your part. You need to be patient, stay the course, and demonstrate your commitment to this new strategy." Consultants are well known for expecting their clients to sit tight for years and have faith that the results will *eventually* happen.

But the way that an initiative gets started is an indicator of how it's likely to perform over time. If it starts slowly and doesn't deliver results from the beginning, it's unlikely to deliver them over a long period of time. How a strategic initiative is executed from the start is critical. You need to demonstrate evidence of success within the first one hundred days. Agile practices help you deliver incremental wins from the start that can be leveraged into larger gains.

THE AGILE MINDSET

The world discovered agile practices out of necessity in response to a growing crisis. Technology companies had failed time and again to release products on time, despite massive investment and resources. Most importantly, perhaps, by the time these products were launched, they were no longer leading edge. The original designs were simply outdated by the time the products were built. By the turn of the century, there was a growing need for a faster and more reliable way to create technology products.

Becoming agile is as much a mindset as it is using a set of practices and tools.

In February 2001, a group of seventeen free thinkers and organizational anarchists met for a relaxed time to talk and ski at The Lodge at Snowbird resort in the Wasatch mountains of Utah. Over cups of coffee, they shared common frustrations and experimental ideas, and eventually put together what became known as the *Agile Software Development Manifesto*.

Over the ensuing years, agility has evolved from a radical movement into a formal discipline. Yet, truly becoming agile is as much a mindset as it is using a set of practices and tools. It really starts by adopting and embracing the philosophy. The agile mindset requires a fundamentally different way of thinking. The following are the key tenets:

- People over processes

- Pace over perfection

- Communication over contracts

- Teamwork over structure

- Iterative instead of all at once

People over processes means that personal relationships, in-person communication, and daily interaction are favored over following prescribed processes.

Pace over perfection emphasizes the importance of getting things done over needing to have everything done perfectly.

Communication over contracts moves away from producing deliverables to meet contract requirements in favor of learning and understanding clients' evolving needs and meeting those needs as they arise.

Teamwork over structure points to the need to network with the people who are critical to getting something done over managing work through a hierarchy.

Iterative instead of all at once, in terms of being agile, means work is done in rapid cycles, responding to change on a continual basis over following a plan, because the plan *is* to regularly iterate.

THE AGILE APPROACH IN ACTION

Agile practices are a time-phased, iterative approach to delivering meaningful outputs incrementally from the start. There is a set of five core practices and tools that will help you adopt agile practices:

1. Turning epics into stories

2. Working in sprints

3. Holding regular scrums

4. Using a Kanban board

5. Working in squads

1. TURNING EPICS INTO STORIES

Plans quickly become obsolete, but planning is essential. We're all familiar with how traditional project management breaks down the work into sequential phases, such as gathering customer requirements, designing, developing, testing, and deploying. Each phase takes place after the previous one over several months. Toward the end of the project, we are finally able to see a working prototype of the finished product. By this time, however, changes in requirements can cause serious delays and expensive rework. Moreover, delays in an earlier phase push the entire project schedule forward.

To solve this, the agile approach combines all these phases into short-term cycles of interactive planning, designing, developing, testing, and deploying. At the end of each cycle, the client can see working prototypes of the end product, give feedback, then see a revised version. Customer input is the next cycle. Change is welcomed at every stage, even late in the process, as a way to incrementally approach the desired result.

Agile projects break down the work into iterative chunks, not sequential phases. One of these chunks is often called the epic, the entire and completed initiative, which may take several months. Epics can be further broken down into stories, which are components of the initiative that can be completed within four to eight weeks and deliver a meaningful output. Stories are further broken down into sprints, which are time-bound cycles of no more than one to two weeks that produce a usable deliverable.

Within each individual sprint, the team looks at all aspects of the project, including requirements, design, development, testing, and deployment to produce a working prototype of the ultimate solution. The project is planned at the epic level and the work gets done at the sprint level. This brings intense focus not on the status of the long-term plan, but on the short-term execution of each cycle.

2. WORKING IN SPRINTS

The sprint is how agile projects get things done in time-bound chunks of work lasting not more than one to two weeks. The sprint is a cycle of focused work to produce a usable deliverable or component. Typically, a sprint team involves people that would naturally need to work together to get something done. This is an ad hoc team, usually of five to nine people.

The agile team starts a sprint by holding a sprint planning session. During sprint planning, the agile team outlines everything that needs to be done within the sprint cycle and each person assigns the tasks to themselves. This is very important. Unlike traditional projects where a manager assigns tasks to individuals, agile team members come up with what needs to be done and then take on the tasks in a free-flowing negotiation among the individuals on the team.

Then the team members assign the number of hours they estimate it's going to take to do each one of those individual tasks. Some agile teams measure the actual hours needed to accomplish a task, while others describe the estimated size of each task as small, medium, large, or extra-large, with a rough understanding of the translation between the size of the task and the number of hours it will take to complete.

Following time estimation, the team reviews the workload to ensure it can be completed within the sprint duration. The scope of work to be done in a sprint can be negotiated, but the sprint duration remains fixed. Agile teams work best when adhering to a constant sprint cycle time. With the agile approach, you keep the time fixed and flex the scope.

To visualize progress within a sprint, the agile team uses a burn down chart that shows the days allotted to the sprint and the total number of work hours estimated to complete that sprint. As individuals accomplish their tasks, they just account for the hours they burn down toward the last day of the sprint. If you notice that it is taking longer to complete tasks than you anticipated, you don't extend the length of the sprint, but instead figure out how to scale back what you're going to do so you can still deliver a meaningful output by the end of the sprint.

3. HOLDING REGULAR SCRUMS

Once the sprint planning is done, agile project teams meet regularly in fifteen-to-twenty-minute stand-up meetings called scrums. During a scrum, everyone in the agile team is standing up to report progress and plan the next few days' work. Most agile teams hold daily scrums, although some meet less frequently, usually at the same time of the day for consistency.

In rugby, a scrum is where the entire team locks themselves shoulder to shoulder to push against the other team to capture the ball. In the agile approach, a scrum is a team huddle. Everyone stands in a semicircle, facing a board showing the work that is currently in progress. The scrum is facilitated by a scrum master, not a manager, who ensures every team member reports on what they did in the last day or two, what they're working on at the time, and what they're doing in the next few days. Every person states whether they're on time, ahead of, or behind schedule, and whether they need something from another team member.

The idea is that, within fifteen to twenty minutes, everyone coordinates what needs to be done and walks away with a clear game plan for the next day or two. The scrum conversation is purely a process checkpoint—nothing else! So, typical questions are: "What did you do yesterday?" "What are you doing today?" "What is your situation?"

The object is to very quickly coordinate with your teammates. If a conversation looks like it's going to take longer than a few minutes, you deal with it outside the scrum conversation. The scrum master is to ensure that the scrum doesn't turn into a problem-solving conversation. This is to be a lightning-fast round of reviews, so, by the end, everyone has a clear game plan.

People outside the project team are invited to attend and observe scrums—but *only to observe* the proceedings; they are not to participate in the conversation. By doing that, observers get an instant update on where the project is. It's a clear window into the status of the team and its project.

4. USING A KANBAN BOARD

The Kanban board is a tool to show how each task is progressing during the sprint. *Kanban* is a Japanese word that refers to the concept of focusing on one, or just a few, things at a time. In the agile practices, a Kanban board allows a team to focus on what they have to do between scrums. The Kanban board typically displays five columns:

- Backlog: All the tasks that need to be done on the project

- To Do: The prioritized tasks to be accomplished in the current sprint

- Doing: The tasks to be accomplished by the next scrum

- Verify: Tasks that are completed but need to be verified that they are done

- Done: Completed tasks

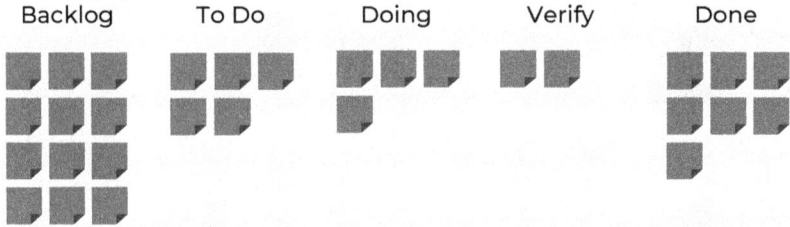

Figure 8.1

By moving a task from column to column, you clearly see how the work is flowing from the backlog to the to-do list for the sprint, what's being done at the moment, and what's been accomplished. The team is fully responsible for getting every task done by the last day of the sprint—either done or repositioned into the backlog, because it's been found to be out of scope for the current sprint.

To add a level of accountability, you can create swim lanes on the Kanban board for each individual on the project team, showing how their work is progressing. If someone is getting overloaded, you can move a task from one swim lane to the lane of someone who is willing to pick up the task and help their teammate move forward. The Kanban board helps you visualize the current work in progress and the interdependencies between teammates. This fosters peer accountability and also ensures that people get the help they need, when they need it.

5. WORKING IN SQUADS

A squad is a group of agile teams operating in concert as part of a larger agile organization.

The squad leader sets an overarching goal and prioritizes the work across multiple agile teams. Then the squad leader facilitates the agile teams to self-organize and work autonomously toward the broader goal. A squad is the organizational scaled-up version of an agile team.

When you're a member of a squad, it's like being part of a start-up company. Everyone contributes as part of a team toward a common goal. While focused on a goal, the squad takes precedence over an individual's functional discipline. Hierarchical lines become blurred or disappear completely, because the squad is where agile team members spend most of their time during the life of a squad's project.

A squad may include people from multiple disciplines, each working within one or more agile teams. The squad will work intensely together for a period of time to get something done. When the project is done, the squad dissolves and the members may join other squads. As a work unit, the squad is intended to be temporary.

Multiple squads may be part of a tribe, a larger cross-functional group that shares common goals. Everyone working on a product may be in a tribe, on a specific squad that creates a particular function of that product, and within the squad participating in a few agile teams to deliver specific components.

The agile vocabulary is still new and experimental in the life of most organizations. Organizations at the entry levels of the agility maturity curve are simply experimenting with agile practices and tools on an as-needed basis. Agile practices are championed by one or two individuals, while use of agile practices is unfamiliar to most.

As the agile approach starts gaining momentum and people start recognizing its value, organizations move up the agile maturity curve to where they have several agile subject-matter experts and possibly several agile teams making consistent use of agile practices and tools. The agile approach starts to measure the speed, quality, and reliability of execution.

As an organization continues to evolve along the agile maturity curve, agility becomes an organizing force. At this point, they are starting to operate around the agile concepts at the enterprise level. Ultimately, the agile mindset becomes the prevailing culture and the natural way of doing things.

We are at a point in organizational history where few organizations are high on the agile maturity curve. But there are many moving up that curve quickly. Even many large corporations are beginning to realize that the agile approach can provide a competitive advantage, something that, if done effectively, will enable them to outperform their competition in ways that will be very hard for those competitors to replicate.

* * *

At eight o'clock in the morning, the lights were still off. No one was around. Was this a workday? By nine, a few employees had gathered at the company kitchen for a cup of coffee. By ten, work began. People were firing up their workstations. And then, within a few minutes, everyone was working frantically. Lots of activity! Plenty of energy! But, in fact, little progress was being made toward the company's critical product release.

This innovative New York City technology start-up had big aspirations, but its reality was lagging far behind. Their quest was to automate digital marketing through personalized content powered by proprietary artificial intelligence. The young founders of the enterprise had quickly found themselves at the head of a fast-growing company at the leading edge of technology with an expanding customer base and growing expectations in the market.

They'd had all-night coding sessions. Produced a prototype. Delivered a great demo to their investors. All of that gave them a great start, but much more was required now. What had worked for them in the early stages of the start-up was no longer carrying them along. And, before this, not one of the founders had ever managed more than five people, let alone an organization rapidly growing to more than two hundred employees!

Most decisions were made by the company's executives. Everyone acted as if they reported directly to one of those executives. And, even after adding a few seasoned executives, most of the workforce was young and inexperienced, so few of them could answer the many questions that came up constantly. Many simply didn't even know what questions to ask.

Consequently, the work sprawled in all directions. Without a clear decision-making process, people were chasing multiple tasks. Plagued with too many competing priorities, everyone was in survival mode. While the work *was* getting done, it was extremely labor intensive, prone to errors, and highly unpredictable.

To help them get a handle on their work, I introduced this organization to agile practices. For the engineering team, this meant creating a product roadmap, so everyone could understand the big picture and have clear goals. The roadmap became a large graphic display on a wall that everyone could see, write on, and edit as needed. With a roadmap in place, we then identified milestones. We broke down all development projects into agile components: epics, themes, stories, and sprints. This allowed the engineering team to set realistic goals for the year, the next quarter, the current month, and the next two weeks.

We put the engineering team's focus squarely on the current two-week sprint. Delivering on their sprint goal became everyone's number-one priority. To ensure that they could deliver, we defined and tracked the tasks that would be done just within the next one to two days. This goal-setting hierarchy immediately helped the engineers focus on priorities while keeping in mind the connection between their daily tasks and the big picture.

To manage multiple strategic projects simultaneously, we organized the engineering department into seven agile teams consisting of cross-functional experts. Agile team members included a core group plus a few additional members who were pulled in ad hoc, based on the need for their expertise. Each agile team met every two weeks to set sprint goals. Then, they met daily for ten-minute stand-up scrums to report on progress and coordinate the work for the day.

To help visualize what everyone was working on, we built Kanban boards—initially, large whiteboards on wheels, filled with three-by-five-inch cards that laid out each person's tasks inside a horizontal swim lane across the to-do, doing, and done columns. The visibility of these large whiteboards with tasks moving across them inspired accountability. Eventually, these boards evolved into large electronic displays mounted in sight of everyone on the company floor.

Not everyone was immediately on board with this approach. At one critical point, a team leader refused to write down every single task on a card, just to have it displayed on the board. "What's the point?" he demanded. "I don't have time to write each task on a card." The CTO calmly replied that he would like to know what the leader and his team were working on. In frustration, this team leader hastily scribbled several cards with lots of tasks. "There you have it," he said as he posted the cards on the board.

The CTO stepped forward and read every single card the team leader had posted. Then he asked, "Are you going to do all of these things in the next two weeks?"

The team leader looked puzzled. "Well, not all of them. Some may take a lot longer than that."

To which the CTO replied, "All you need to do is post the tasks you'll do in the next two weeks." When the team leader was finished, only a few cards were left on the board showing what he was committing to over those weeks—a much simpler task than he had made it out to be.

To further highlight the status of the various projects, and of the individual agile team members, we assigned color codes: red, yellow, and green. No one wanted to be highlighted in red for long. Everyone strove to keep their tasks moving steadily forward in green. This public display of accountability became so important to the company that eventually a display was placed in the company's lobby, so even *customers* could see at a glance, in real time, how product development was progressing! Agile practices quickly focus everyone's energies on delivering the most critical tasks that need to get done. That's the power of agile practices!

Agile practices quickly focus everyone's energies on delivering the most critical tasks that need to get done.

---

* * *

I've heard many people say, "Well, this all works well in the high-tech world, but how is it going to work for us?" The agile process can be adapted to deliver similar value across all kinds of organizations. Let's quickly look at an example in the construction industry.

At a construction site, lots of unexpected things can happen that are not according to plan. Weather conditions affect schedules. Crews may have members with varying skills and aptitudes for doing the work. Equipment may malfunction, or materials may be delayed or incorrect. And there are many interdependencies across teams that work for different companies and follow different priorities. How can you expect a construction crew to become agile?

It's six o' clock in the morning. I open the trailer door, and the crew is gathered, ready to start the day. Stapled on the back of the trailer door is a Kanban board. The foreman explains what needs to get done during that day. Each crew member or two picks a section of a wall, a floor, or a roof they'll work on. The foreman says everyone will get off early if they get all of these tasks done, but the day is not over until they get it all done. If the sprint is done by Friday, he adds, there'll be a steak dinner for everyone, on the company.

Just that simple. And due to this approach, the project is moving steadily ahead of schedule. Morale is high. Teamwork and collaboration are flourishing across the various crews working on the site. This is an agile project.

The general contractor includes project managers from the different companies involved in the construction project in the process of planning each sprint. Everything is coordinated to the hour. Everyone knows their part and the impact their work will have on others. If they get the sprint done on time, there is a bonus for each company. If they are late, there is a penalty for all of the companies.

Every section of the project that is part of the current sprint is carefully planned. The focus is on getting that piece of the project done right and on time. The rest of the project is outlined as well, but not actively managed until its sprint begins.

The contractor broke down the entire project into the main themes. Then they broke down the themes into stories, and stories into sprints. Within the theme for the building's foundation, for example, they had stories such as site test, excavation, framing of the foundation, pouring of the concrete, and, finally, the curing and finishing of the foundation. Everyone needed to know what they are doing and what others needed from them and by when. With this understanding, they could operate as a team.

Agile practices helped reverse a tendency at this construction company toward projects going over budget and often losing money. Using the agile approach, the company drastically increased its ability to deliver large complex projects on time and on budget—in some cases, earning a premium for being done ahead of schedule. In addition, agile practices lifted morale, increased teamwork, and advanced quality and safety.

KEY TAKEAWAYS

- Agile practices are the next step in strategic transformation after selecting the right people, setting the organizational structure and defining work processes.
- Agile practices are a time-phased, iterative approach to delivering meaningful outputs incrementally from the start.
- The key tenets of the agile mindset are:
  - People over processes
  - Pace over perfection
  - Communication over contracts
  - Teamwork over structure
  - Iterative instead of all at once

- The five core practices and tools that will help you adopt agile practices are:
  - Turning epics into stories
  - Working in sprints
  - Holding regular scrums
  - Using a Kanban board
  - Working in squads

CHAPTER NINE

ENGAGE—BRINGING OUT THE BEST IN OTHERS

When the people become fully engaged in doing their best work, their drive, energy, and enthusiasm transform the organization.

Are you fully engaged at work? If so, how can you create the conditions to engage others? We perform at our best when we are fully engaged in something we truly care about. Anything less than full engagement falls short of reaching peak performance. Sports athletes, artistic performers, and accomplished professionals all know what it is like to do something you love doing—it feels great!

While the concept of "employee engagement" is relatively new, the idea behind it is not. For decades, attempts to define employees' discretionary efforts at work have been described with words such as productivity, job satisfaction, employee morale, initiative, and empowerment. Engagement is a contemporary, comprehensive measure for doing one's best at work.

While engagement is always desired and valuable, the need for full engagement comes at a very specific time in the strategic transformation process. If you focus on it too early during a transformation—before you have strategy, structure, and processes in place—you may generate a lot of excitement and build up motivation that you may not be able to maintain.

If people are not clear about direction, or priorities constantly change, or the organization is not structured properly and you will be reorganizing, or if the processes are not well defined and people don't have effective ways of working together, creating engagement may quickly turn into frustration as expectations cannot be met. For example, if you need to reorganize, you may have to replace or move around some people, and you want to engage them once they are where they will actually be working.

High engagement happens when the needs and wants of both the organization and the employees are met. In order to be engaged, a person must be satisfied, motivated, and competent—all three. Just having one or the other of these qualities isn't enough.

When the people become fully engaged in doing their best work, their drive, energy, and enthusiasm transform the organization.

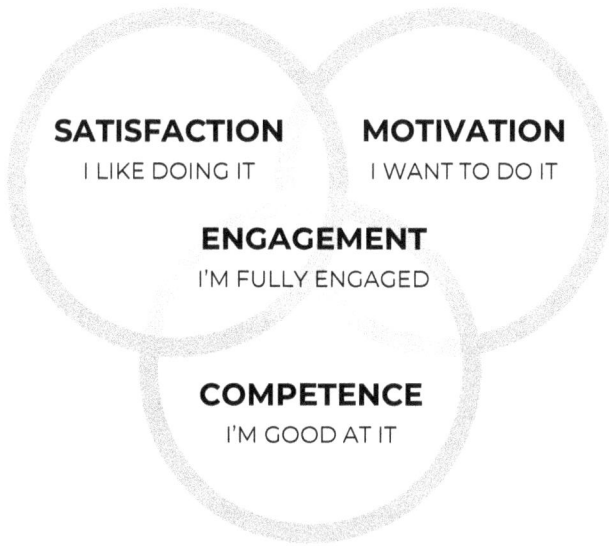

Figure 9.1

Most people only have one or two of these elements in their jobs, but to be *fully* engaged they need all three. To do our best work, we need to like the work, want to do it, and be good at it. As a leader, you must capture your employees' hands, hearts, and minds. The hands represent satisfaction with the work itself. The heart represents the motivation for doing the work. The mind represents the desire to do the work well. When people have all three of those elements on the job, they're all in.

Take, for example, an assembly line worker who is satisfied with her job. Her job means steady employment, a secure paycheck, and a convenient work schedule, which is motivating. But she is not one of the best workers and doesn't exert herself beyond what's strictly necessary. She may be satisfied and motivated, but unless she is also effective, she's not fully engaged.

Her coworker has recently been given the assignment to ensure the assembly line is producing at record capacity. She is highly effective in this role and has been able to boost production targets.

This challenge has made her job very motivating. But her manager rarely recognizes her good work, so she is unhappy with her boss and is looking for a different job. She is effective and motivated, but unless she is also satisfied, she is not fully engaged.

A third coworker has just been hired. She is still learning the job, so she is not highly effective yet. But she is satisfied with her pay and thoroughly enjoys having a job so she can pay off bills. She tries to maximize her hours and do what is needed. She is satisfied and highly motivated, and once she becomes effective, she will become fully engaged.

In order to be fully engaged, employees need to be doing work that they enjoy doing, work they are good at, and work that meets their needs. And, of course, the organization needs that type of work to meet its goals as well. This chapter describes how to create the conditions to fully engage others to do their best work.

It is important to recognize that engagement is not an all-or-nothing thing. There are different degrees and levels of engagement; in a particular situation, we may experience different levels of engagement. This leads most people to assume that their engagement is controlled by external factors outside their control. It's as if we expect someone to come and fix what's bothering us so we can be fully engaged. We may feel justified to be less than fully engaged given the circumstances.

The fact is that, while we can't control external factors, our attitude *is* our choice. The level of engagement we experience at work is largely driven by us. It's a choice. Certainly, the choice can be facilitated or hindered by external factors.

Let's review the different levels of engagement:

- Fully engaged: loves the work, is constantly learning, takes calculated risks, feels stretched beyond the comfort zone, takes satisfaction in the quality of the work

- Engaged: in general likes the job, is willing to learn, feels cooperative and helpful, is committed to what it takes to get things done, supports the organization's leadership in the organization

- Passively engaged: does what is necessary, sticks to what is known, takes few risks, rarely feels stretched, puts in the time, does what's necessary to get paid, not unhappy but also not excited

- Passively disengaged: does only what is necessary to get by and not get in trouble, doesn't contribute to full capacity, spends time at work taking care of personnel needs, can be hard to work with

- Actively disengaged: bored and frustrated, makes sarcastic jokes about work, speaks negatively about the company and the leaders, looks for ways to find blame, makes accusations, punishes themselves and others by mentally quitting but physically staying at work

What is your level of engagement at work? And what can you do to bring yourself and others to a higher engagement? The payoff for doing this is well worth the effort.

> *Choose a job you love, and you will never*
> *have to work a day in your life.*
>
> —*attributed to Confucius*

* * *

While operating more than four hundred restaurants across the United States, El Pollo Loco executives noticed that only a handful of their restaurants consistently excelled across all performance measures—and by a significant margin. They thought that if they could identify and replicate what made these few restaurants so successful, they could help all their other restaurants as well.

They began by looking at the typical success factors in their industry: location, size, and competition. To their surprise, the top-performing properties did not necessarily enjoy the benefits of a great location, or ample footprint, or little competition. In fact, some of the best ones had once been among the worst performers until a new manager took over. They wondered if the manager could be the secret sauce. They asked me to find out. My job was to assess what made top-performing El Pollo Loco restaurants so much more successful than the others.

El Pollo Loco is a fast-growing, quick-service restaurant chain specializing in lime-infused grilled chicken. At peak hours, any one of their top restaurants was buzzing with customers. Orders moved fast. The workers were serving customers quickly and efficiently and with a flair for having a good time. The general impression was welcoming, fun, and friendly. And the manager was orchestrating a positive experience for these workers by constantly reinforcing them. He pointed out and celebrated every little thing they did right. Following the manager's lead, crew members also built each other up, and they served their customers with competence and a smile.

Not that everything always went right, but the manager dealt with that too—quickly and constructively. During slow times, the crew would huddle at a table and go over everything they'd done right or wrong. Everything in the restaurant was analyzed, from the length of the queue for orders to the condition of the salsa bar to the cleanliness of the bathrooms. If someone had let others down, it was brought out in the open without either mincing words or creating ill feelings. The employees just saw it as feedback to help them do their jobs better. The feedback was specific and direct, but the overall tone was always positive and reassuring.

I discovered that high-engagement restaurants like this one produced 10 percent higher sales, 30 percent higher customer satisfaction ratings, and 15 percent less turnover than similarly located units. Even more interesting was my finding that high-engagement restaurant managers were able to bring their sizzle to any new restaurant they went to, reproducing similar success within six to nine months. Employee engagement, we discovered, was primarily a function of the manager.

Armed with this insight, El Pollo Loco set out to establish employee engagement as part of their formula for success. The engagement process started with listening to employees define engagement on their own terms. Managers found, for example, that what engages restaurant crew members is vastly different from what engages office staff employees. The company then trained regional leaders and restaurant managers on engagement principles and practices, using as models the managers who had mastered those principles. They reinforced the training with engagement workshops at each restaurant and a recognition program.

In three years, El Pollo Loco significantly increased employee engagement, which contributed to it becoming one of the fastest-growing and most successful restaurant chains in the nation.

WHAT ENGAGEMENT IS AND WHAT DRIVES IT

Think about a time when you were feeling engaged in doing something, something you enjoyed doing so much that you lost yourself in the activity. You didn't really have a sense of time. You had boundless energy. You were extremely creative. You were loving what you were doing, so it didn't feel like work anymore. You found yourself performing at your very best and felt satisfied just doing the activity, not focusing on the result. That's what it feels like to be fully engaged.

Most people would say that those are optimal experiences in life, which they can only find in hobbies or sports or some other activity they do outside of work. But some people experience this in the workplace. As a transformational leader, you can create a workplace that more consistently produces an environment where people can be fully engaged—and therefore be more creative and productive. As the leader, your task is to create a work culture that brings out the best in others. And you do this by understanding the drivers of engagement, improving your own emotional intelligence, and resolving conflicts in a proactive and positive way.

As the leader, your task is to create a work culture that brings out the best in others.

On my way to the top floor of a company that had been recognized as one of the best places to work, I immediately noticed the vibe. It was like a supercharged feeling of excitement about starting the day. Listening to employees who were coming from the cafeteria with their cups of coffee and breakfast food and going up to their desks, you could clearly sense that they were ready to get down to work.

The casual elevator conversations were about how time was of the essence, how they were going to barely get their work done by the end of the day, how the day was going to be over before they knew it. They all conveyed the sense that it was "game day" and that they were walking onto the field to compete. Noticeably, as the elevator doors opened at every floor, people came in and out ready to give their best.

Not all elevator rides feel the same. In some companies, the chat is about the weekend—the past one or the one coming. Or about what they do outside of work—hobbies, family, and personal travel plans. In other companies, the elevator is a cone of silence, a place where people stare away from each other while waiting to exit. It's as if they are serving time and they are bracing for what happens once the elevator doors open.

Which elevator ride best describes the culture of your organization? And what can you do to create a highly engaged work culture?

Culture can be described as the operating system of an organization: it's always running, it underlies everything in the system, it affects the way everything and everyone works—or doesn't work. Culture is what drives organizational performance. So working on your culture should be an ongoing effort. Just as upgrading your computer operating system will enhance the performance of all your tools and applications, upgrading your culture to a higher level of engagement will enhance the performance of all the people in your organization.

To build the desired culture, the transformation leader starts by identifying and modeling the desired behaviors. Not everyone is motivated by the same things. It is important to identify the behaviors that will have the greatest impact on engagement. Every person, team, and organization is more likely to be fully engaged by different behaviors.

For example, partners at a law firm may be fully engaged by attractive advancement opportunities in a highly competitive environment, while nurses at a hospital may be fully engaged by being treated with dignity and respect while having the equipment and procedures to serve patients. Entrepreneurial company employees are usually engaged by an innovative, fast-paced work environment that tolerates risks and rewards upside opportunities, while scientific lab workers may value job security, long-term career tracks, and interesting assignments.

It is up to you, as the transformation leader, to identify the behaviors that bring out the best in the people in your organization. Then you start modeling such behaviors consistently. Your example starts creating an environment where the best people get noticed and recognized, and consistently excel. As you recognize those who are displaying the desired behaviors, consistent individual behaviors turn into personal habits, which inform collective patterns of conduct, which over time shape the norms for the desired culture.

THE POWER OF RECOGNITION

Leading by example is powerful, and it cannot be delegated. As the leader, you *are* the culture. The organizational culture is an extension of your leadership qualities. What you do, right or wrong, defines what's acceptable. Start noticing what behaviors are helping or hurting the desired culture. Recognize your influence as a leader and start working on yourself first.

As you focus on modeling the desired behaviors, pay attention to others who are doing the right things, too, and point that out. Let them know that you notice when they do something right. Recognition is the next most powerful way to influence behavior. Unfortunately, it is also least used by most managers. The best El Pollo Loco managers knew how to use recognition effectively.

Recognition means catching people doing things right and letting them know. When people feel valued for what they are doing, they will try to do it more often. There are many ways you can do this. The obvious one is to say thank you. It doesn't cost anything and it doesn't take much time, but sincere appreciation always goes a long way.

Recognition means catching people doing things right and letting them know. When people feel valued for what they are doing, they will try to do it more often.

Verbal recognition is powerful. Some people prefer to receive a personal message in private, while others thrive on public recognition among peers. You can also use rewards as a way to recognize people, but keep in mind that paying for a behavior cheapens and ultimately undermines the behavior. When recognizing with a gift, it is best to use nonmonetary perks such as a paid lunch, gift card, or special parking spot.

One company thanks employees with a paid day off in recognition for dedication and effort. Another company sends high-performing employees to leadership courses or educational opportunities to show that they value learning. Some companies like to recognize with perks to show that rewards matter. To be most effective, the recognition needs to be aligned with the organization's values and tailored to what will produce the best results for the employee. Organizations that fail to make this connection have unintentionally punished people through their rewards.

Managers can be encouraged to recognize others. At one company, managers are given discretionary resources to reward high-performing employees. Surprisingly, only five managers *out of several hundred* actually rewarded people consistently. And those five managers were the most loved and appreciated, the kind whose employees would do anything for them. They were superstars in the organization, and they became superstars by giving stars to other people.

While recognition focuses on catching people doing the right things, it doesn't mean that you need to ignore problems. Candid and respectful feedback is critical to creating a healthy culture. Instead of seeing feedback as a negative, critical, or uncomfortable communication, transformational leaders need to make it a positive experience about learning, growing, and improving.

The successful El Pollo Loco managers knew what they needed to do to engage their employees through consistent positive reinforcement. But they also showed great skill at providing critical feedback without making it personal. Those managers set an expectation that if an employee was not all in, delivering the highest-quality service to the customer and working well with fellow employees, they would be out.

Instead of trying to force the person into a standard they could not meet, they simply addressed the problem as a lack of fit with the culture. "I'm running a top-performing restaurant," the manager would say, "so I need top-performing staff. If you are not interested in being a top performer, I will help you find a job where you can be a good fit." He meant it literally and would help low-performing staff get a job at another nearby restaurant. There would be no room for low performers in the team. If the employee wasn't up to the standard, the manager would let that employee go—gently but decisively. The terms were so cordial that the departing member was invited to come back once they were ready to be part of the team.

In order to create an environment to attract and retain the best people, a leader must create the conditions for full engagement. In order to do that, the leader must understand how his or her own attitudes, words, and actions are perceived by others.

LEADING ONLINE AT A DISTANCE

As I write this book in the midst of the COVID-19 pandemic, we are living in times of unprecedented change. In a matter of a few weeks, the entire world changed in drastic and unimaginable ways. Faster than most of us could fully grasp the implications, most of the world entered a new reality of pandemic, quarantine, work from home, lockdowns, wearing face masks, and takeout services.

While we can't fully predict the short- and long-term effects of this new normal, one thing we know for sure: it is different. We are now making major global decisions by the numbers. We are experiencing personal conversations, regular meetings, large-scale events, and social gatherings online through a screen. We are familiar operating from kitchen tables, bedroom desks, drive-by windows, and curbsides.

As with every shift, there are some deep and lasting consequences that are not necessarily obvious. What are the implications for leading in this emerging online, socially distant world? And, more importantly, what can you do to remain relevant and influential?

LEADING IN A DIGITAL HIERARCHY

In some ways, we have been preparing for this next step for decades. The advent of the computer, the internet, email, instant messaging and social media have been preparing us to manage in a digital space. During the pandemic lockdown, this space is claiming huge amounts of our time.

Most of us are now spending very significant portions of our time online, leveraging all the tools and technologies that keep us connected while apart. This has suddenly shifted our interactions with the traditional hierarchy, because we are all mere digital images coming across on the same computer screen.

Suddenly gone are the social and political impressions of walking into an executive corner office, or walking past the executive assistant to meet with a senior manager, entering into a corporate boardroom lined up with leather chairs. To access anyone, just click on the link and they show up onscreen the exact same way as everyone else. Faced with this equalizing digital interface, what can leaders do to lead, manage, and influence others? What now makes you a respected leader, a rising star, a strong contributor, or even a supportive follower? Deprived of, or limited in our use of the traditional social cues and power symbols, we must learn to manage in this newly significant digital space.

WE ARE ALL CONNECTED WHILE APART

Most of us are now getting used to staying connected through technology while being socially distant from each other. Some companies have been practicing flexible work arrangements with varying degrees of success. Some couples and families have been keeping up their relationship through regular video calls while working away from each other. Many professionals have been working remotely for a while.

Leaders of organizations where a significant portion of the people work remotely keep people focused, motivated, and accountable through structured online interactions similar to the practices of social media influencers. The five key practices for staying connected while apart are:

1. Master interacting through technology platforms

2. Deliver sensory experiences online—it's more than just words

3. Influence by quality and quantity of content

4. Stay relevant by engaging with content—yours or others

5. Present clear and compelling calls to action

Leaders of organizations where a significant portion of the people work remotely keep people focused, motivated, and accountable through structured online interactions similar to the practices of social media influencers.

THE CURRENCY OF ONLINE INFLUENCING

Master your platform. Social media influencers have known that success on one or two platforms is far better than mediocrity across many. Likewise, managers need to consistently use and optimize one or two digital communication channels.

Are you excellent at email or just acceptable? Are you amazing on video conferencing or is it just a "you get what you get" show? Are you leveraging instant messaging or is it just a sideline channel? Are you posting fresh and relevant content regularly, or just responding to others' content?

The answer to these questions reveals to what extent you are leveraging digital technologies as a way to influence. Most leaders are simply users of media channels and not strategic masters of the media. Leaders who strategically use the most popular media channels have gained significant influence.

Take, for example, the last two US presidential campaigns. Candidate Barack Obama leveraged email and text messaging during his presidential campaign to reach millions, influence public opinion, and connect with millions across the country. He did this to a significantly greater extent than his political opponent and won the election. Likewise, candidate Donald Trump demonstrated dexterity with tweets. Mastering the media channels people are most familiar with is key to digital leadership.

BUILDING YOUR AUDIENCE

As a digital workplace manager, think like a social media influencer. Ask yourself, what would a social media influencer do to reach, engage, and influence followers?

Start thinking of the people you lead as an audience. In uncertain times, most people are seeking clarity, information, inspiration, validation, and reinforcement. Whether the message comes from you or someone else, people are seeking relevant content to do their work more effectively.

As a digital workplace leader, ask yourself:

- What information do they need from me?

- What is their level of awareness of my priorities?

- What about my message is timely and engaging?

- What specific call to action do I want them to respond to?

- What is the best way to deliver that information?

- How often would they be willing and able to receive it?

RESIDUAL EFFECTS AFTER GETTING BACK TO WORK

What the working experience will look like after quarantine is anyone's guess. We hope to get back to work, to in-person meetings, to social events and gatherings. We might find a significant number of people will continue to work remotely. We might continue to leverage technology in new and innovative ways. We might experience residual effects or discover unexpected benefits from the digital experience.

Digital leadership will require dexterity with prevailing media channels. Digital leaders need to build an audience. The quality and quantity of content matters. Your messages will determine the level of awareness, engagement, and action from those who interact with you. Digital leadership is about being always present while staying apart.

KEY TAKEAWAYS

- Only when we are fully engaged can we reach peak performance. A fully engaged culture is a high performing culture.

- High engagement happens when the needs and wants of both the organization and the employees are met. In order to be engaged, a person must be satisfied, motivated, and competent—all three.

- You create a work culture that brings out the best in others by understanding the drivers of engagement, improving your own emotional intelligence, and learning how to resolve conflicts that can poison the culture.

- There can be quite a difference between what engages the people in one kind of profession or role versus those in another kind of profession or role, but there is one way of engaging people that is common to almost everyone: recognition.

- Emotional intelligence is the ability to recognize your own emotions and those of others and use emotional information to guide thinking and behavior.

- A leader needs to recognize that conflict is a learning opportunity, a way to achieve better alignment or greater understanding—and even for building greater engagement.

CHAPTER TEN

MEASURE—ACHIEVING GOALS BY MEASURING PERFORMANCE

Most people measure activities while expecting results, but if you want to achieve results, you need to measure performance, not progress.

We spend significant time focused on doing things hoping that they will lead to the desired result. Often we get lost in doing so many things that we shift our focus away from the goal. This makes the desired result unattainable, simply because it's not aligned to our actions.

The logic is that in order to achieve a goal, we must do certain things. So we get busy doing the things that we hope will ultimately lead to achieving the goal. In the process, our focus tends to shift into measuring progress by the tasks we are completing instead of measuring performance against achieving the goal.

Activities come easy. They are tangible, concrete, and manageable. They keep people busy. We get a sense of accomplishment as we list and complete tasks. Most people like to report their contributions by the projects they have completed. They find satisfaction in checking things off their to-do lists.

But to deliver results you must *focus on results, not activities*. The activity mindset measures and reports on things such as the amount of time spent on the job, the number of calls made, the reports done, the emails sent, the meetings attended. Measuring such things may make it seem like people are making progress and being productive. But if you look at it closely—and objectively—you may find that too few of these activities lead directly to achieving goals.

To deliver results you must focus on achieving goals, not on completing activities.

People who focus on results set goals and track progress by measuring performance—not what is *done*, but what those actions are actually *accomplishing*. They measure performance indicators to identify the ones with the highest impact on the result, and they constantly adjust their performance to reach the goal.

This chapter focuses on achieving results by setting meaningful goals, measuring performance, and consistently hitting targets that directly affect goal achievement.

* * *

Several years ago, I started competing in triathlons as a way to stay fit. My goal was to finish a race in the top ten of my age group. It was a clear, simple goal. I broke down that goal into objectives that involved training extensively—swimming, biking, and running for up to ten hours a week. When I entered my first triathlon, I was very excited and felt good throughout, but at the end I was surprised to find my name listed at the bottom of my age group in the results.

So I renewed the commitment to my goal and started to train harder. I extended my workout to fourteen hours a week, bought racing gear, read triathlon training books. But, despite all of this, race after race I found my name listed at the bottom of the finishers in my age group. I thought to myself, *I just may not be that good at this sport*. But I didn't give up. I spent nearly six years preparing for and competing in triathlons, but there was never any significant change in my race results.

Finally, I decided to discuss my situation with a triathlon coach. After listening to my story, he quickly said, "Let me guess: you can finish each race with a smile on your face, but you are nowhere near the top ten finishers."

"Exactly!" I said, shocked that he had guessed my plight so easily.

He said, "The problem is, you've been measuring effort instead of performance. Training time is effort, running speed is performance. You're clearly in good shape, well trained. What you need to do now is measure your performance against the top ten finishers and shoot for their level."

We looked it up right then and found that the top ten finishers in my age group were biking at twenty-one miles an hour consistently versus my seventeen miles an hour, and they were running seven-minute miles to my ten-minute miles. The coach told me to work on running and biking at their pace. That very week, I changed my training approach. I focused only on the race pace required to finish in the top ten. That Saturday, *just a week after talking to the coach*, I placed ninth in my age group at a triathlon. In the next triathlon, I came in sixth, and in the very next one, I was *on the podium*, having placed third in my age group!

It was amazing. I was consistently achieving top-ten race results while training fewer hours and putting in less effort. I was working smarter, rather than harder, simply by measuring and working on the right factors, the ones that delivered results.

* * *

Intentionally or by default, what we measure sets the focal point for actions that produce predictable outcomes. To give another example, a person may want to become more physically fit by losing weight. But weight loss is a poor performance measure for physical fitness. Food intake and amount of exercise are more directly linked to the goal of physical fitness and therefore are more likely to produce fitness than will obsessing about weight loss.

What you measure is what you get. Change the measurement and you immediately change the results. Most people measure activities because they are easier to measure, while hoping to reach goals. Measuring *effort* leads to being busy, while measuring *performance* delivers results.

What you measure is what you get. Change the measurement and you immediately change the results.

Many organizations are activity driven, not results driven. They need to switch their focus to *what must be done to improve*, rather than on just *the need for improvement* itself. Switching to a focus on results will reveal what needs to be done to achieve the results. And results should appear from the beginning and happen regularly throughout the process. Goals need to be incremental and manageable, so they produce periodic results on a regular basis. These continual successes are what maintain the pace and energy of your strategic transformation.

THE POWER OF BEING RESULTS DRIVEN

Many times, we pursue goals but do not measure them, or don't measure them correctly. And then we're surprised that achieving the goal seems to be difficult or elusive.

If someone is focused on *results*, they are driven by goal accomplishments. In order to achieve goals, they need to measure, track, and report the right performance indicators. When somebody is focused on *activities*, they track all the things being done, make extensive checklists, and report and celebrate efforts and the completion of activities— which may or may not have contributed to the desired result.

Many organizations' attempts at transformation are activity driven. They have been told that there is a prescribed method, a specific set of actions, to achieve a cultural change or a strategic objective, or to roll out a strategy. People are encouraged to exercise a lot of patience and fortitude, because the change is not going to happen right away. For example, I've heard a claim that cultural change takes two to three years.

So these organizations are told that they have to be very committed and stay the course. Everyone needs to be trained on a common framework and tool kit so they can properly follow and support the change process. And the organizations' customers are required to make big investments in this change and to expect that all their results will come at the end of this long process.

Most of us have seen initiatives that look like this. Unfortunately, they are activity centered and, as a result, are more focused on activities that *work toward the improvement*, instead of starting with the improvement itself and figuring out the specific key steps that will get them to realize the improvement. All the energy goes into measuring and reporting *the things people are doing* rather than the *incremental improvements they should be achieving*. A results-driven improvement focuses on the specific things that people need to do to directly achieve incrementally better results. Everything else is considered superfluous.

A results-driven improvement focuses on the specific things that people need to do to directly achieve incrementally better results.

The leadership in a results-driven organization encourages its people to deliver results quickly, within a month to three months at the most, and to present measurable evidence of improvement on a regular basis. If you engage experts to help you, it should not be because of their methodology or their prescribed approach to doing things, but because they can contribute directly to achieving results, and because they can test and verify what is working, so you can quickly discard what is not working and focus on what is.

A results-oriented approach requires relatively little investment up front and relies on the conviction that the big successes will materialize via ongoing, smaller, incremental successes. When you take this approach, results happen from the beginning, troubleshooting happens quickly, and you see things evolve in the right direction. There is still a methodology, a process, but it simply supports what drives success—that which achieves the desired results. To be results oriented, you need to:

- Set effective goals

- Measure key indicators

- Improve performance

- Report achievements

- Analyze actual results versus goal results

Earlier in the book, I talked about a technology company that was successful for a period of time and then became complacent. They were pursuing too many initiatives, their focus was too spread out, and they were starting to be less successful. I was hired to work with them, and, without making any changes to the leadership in the company or making capital investments, we turned it around in about six months—they ended up having their best year ever, even though their revenue had been *declining* in the first half of the year. Within the next year, they became the industry leader.

How can an organization make such a radical improvement in such a short period of time without changing the leadership or investing capital? A key element to their success was a massive focus on business goals. When I started working with them, they were tracking all the activities that made up the multiple initiatives they were pursuing. The executives and managers were reporting on their to-do lists, on what activities had been completed. But they had little sense of how much progress they were actually making on all these initiatives; there was no clarity about results.

We needed to change that quickly—the company's future depended on it—so we set up a war room and all the executives and managers met there three times a week to report on how their groups were performing against very simple and specific goals. There was a revenue goal, a profitability goal, and an on-time delivery goal. All the executives and managers came to these stand-up meetings and allocated just fifteen to twenty minutes to report how their groups were performing against those measures, what kind of results they were producing. So if you were on a sales team, you reported on revenue; if you were in software development, you reported on delivery time; others reported on how they were contributing to increased profitability.

At first, it was painful for these people to realize that their performance was far off the mark. As they met, day after day, reporting their meager results, it was frustrating for them to realize that they were not on track to meet their goals. In fact, those goals seemed almost unachievable. But, very quickly, people started adjusting their behavior and their focus to concentrate on the measures that really mattered. They chose all of their groups' activities with a focus on achieving those goals. Within a month, the performance metrics started to trend upward. Within three months, they were starting to meet the goals. And within six months, they were actually beginning to *exceed* the goals—they had to establish higher goals because the original ones had already been achieved!

I have been surprised, time and again, by the fact that when an individual or an organization is clearly focused on achieving goals, and is measuring the performance indicators that will lead to achieving those goals, *the goals are relatively easy to achieve*—whether it's me finally finishing in the top ten of a triathlon or a technology company turning itself around within six months. But, in order to find that level of achievement, the individual or organization must set meaningful goals that define success.

SETTING MEANINGFUL GOALS

What do we mean by a goal? As much as organizations and managers talk about goals, the actual definition of a goal is not that clear in most people's minds.

A goal is a measurable long-term achievement. It has to have a number attached to it—if it doesn't, it is probably not a measurable achievement. So in my triathlon experience, my goal was a top-ten finish for my age group. That's easily definable. I could literally draw a line after the tenth person in my age group and say I had finished above or below that line.

A goal is a measurable long-term achievement.

For an organization, the goal could be as simple as getting a certain number of clients, achieving a particular annual revenue number, operating within a target profit margin, winning a percent of market share, or establishing a certain number of clients in a new region. Anything that is measurable, or represents a long-term achievement, can be a goal. Goal setting seems common sense, but it's certainly not common practice.

The problem is that it's often hard to understand how to achieve a goal. My personal goal of finishing in the top ten of a triathlon for my age group would clearly require a level of fitness and physical endurance, but, initially, it was not clear to me what I needed to do to achieve that level. In order to achieve a goal, you need to define objectives. Objectives are specific, short-term accomplishments that will lead you to achieving the goal. So in my case, the objectives that would get me to the goal were to run at a seven-minute mile pace and bike at a twenty-one mile per hour pace.

This is where most people and organizations go wrong. They often misuse the terminology. They refer to their ambition as a goal, but ambition is usually not a goal in the sense that it's not measurable; it's a descriptive end state. My ambition might have been to feel healthy and fit for my age group, but I could have done that in a number of different ways—I didn't have to finish in the top ten of a triathlon to achieve it. Vision is another term that organizations confuse with goal. A vision is much broader. Some organizations substitute initiatives for goals and objectives, and this is where the activity-focused mindset creeps in.

Directions	Vision Our Destination	Mission Our Purpose	Values Our Guiding Principles
	Strategy Concise Statement of Strategic Direction		
Acheivements	Goals High-Level, Long-Term Achievements		Objectives Specific, Near-Term Accomplishments
	Initiatives Actions to Achieve Objectives	Performance Measures Key Performance Indicators (KPIs)	Outcome Measures Indicators of Success
Execution	Strategic Roadmap High-Level Timeline		Operating Plan Year-One Priorities
	Priorities Key Projects and Activities	Deliverables Evidence of Completed Tasks	Progress Reviews Track and Report Progress

Figure 10.1

Holding an organization, a team, or an individual accountable for an objective can be painful, because it means they have to achieve something that requires a real stretch. It's much easier to set an initiative as a goal, because an initiative is something someone can just *do*, and when they complete it say they've achieved their objective—without having to accomplish anything measurable.

Sometimes people use a deliverable as a goal. So if I'm able to submit a deliverable, such as a report, I can believe I've met a goal. If I complete an assignment or hire a new person for my team or do anything else that is a deliverable—a completed task—I can check that off as if I've achieved a goal. When we substitute initiatives or deliverables for goals, we are clearly in the activity mindset, where we can check off all the things on our to-do list, feel good about it, but be nowhere near achieving a real goal.

Surprisingly, there are many organizations—even large corporations with professional management teams—that, instead of defining proper goals and objectives, use initiatives and deliverables. As a result, these organizations do a lot of work, but they can't show the value or impact of that work; they can only show that it's been *done*.

* * *

A high-powered technology start-up had grand aspirations to create the most advanced context-sensitive search engine. This search engine would take into account contextual information about the user to personalize online search—like an intelligent mind reader. To accomplish this vision, they hired a highly innovative technology team. They worked diligently for over two years to bring this product to market. They had made a lot of progress, but they didn't ever seem to be ready to actually launch the product. The CEO of this start-up firm asked me to join their executive team meeting, conduct some observations, and give him recommendations for how they could get the product done and released.

While visiting the company, I immediately observed that they were filled with activity artifacts—project management charts, Kanban boards, and checklists. I also observed that when executives met, everyone reported on a list of activities their groups had accomplished. The marketing team reported on all the things they were doing to prepare for a product launch. The technology team reported on all the things they were doing to develop the product for the launch. This organization was clearly activity driven.

During an executive meeting, when people were dutifully reporting all the things they had done, the CEO turned to me and said, "Juan, can you see that we're working very hard toward this goal?"

I replied, "Toward which goal?"

"Toward the goal of launching the product," he shot back.

"I don't see anywhere a date for releasing the product," I said.

He replied, "Well, we're going to release it when we're ready."

"There's the problem!" I said. "There's no set date that drives everyone and everything toward a release date."

I could see the light spark in the CEO's eyes. The executive team immediately caught the concept. They were working hard, but they all came to the realization that they needed to draw a line in the sand and set a release date—or the product would never be released. With a lot of trepidation, they set the release date for three months in the future.

In response to this date, they reverse-engineered their plans, working backward from the launch date. Some of the features they'd been working on were found to be expendable and fell off the schedule. Some of the marketing campaigns they'd been planning no longer fit the timeline, and much work was eliminated or rescheduled for future releases. Everything had to be prioritized according to the launch date. Needless to say, they made their release date.

WHAT TO MEASURE AND REPORT

The only way to determine if you're progressing toward a goal is to measure what leads to that goal. But all performance measurements are not equally useful, so you need to identify the key indicators. What you measure is what you get. Change what you measure and you change your results.

We've talked about the difference between measuring training time versus speed and pace when trying to finish a race in the top ten, but let's talk about a goal that virtually everyone can relate to: living a healthy life. What do you measure? Most people measure their body weight. That's because it's easy to measure and stands as an outcome of success. We all know, however, that body weight is not a good indicator of health and fitness. Daily calorie intake, eating a balanced diet, sleep, and regular exercise are much better indicators of health and fitness.

Tracking an outcome measure will not improve the result. If you want to be healthy and fit and you focus entirely on measuring body weight, you will become discouraged. Body weight will fluctuate and, as a result, you'll have days where you feel good or bad about your weight. Unless you measure what is affecting body weight, you're only measuring *what has already happened*.

Now, if you started measuring exercise, you might decide to go to the gym three times a week and work out for an hour. Over time, you'd feel like you were building up muscle and consuming more calories. After three months of doing that, you'd probably notice that you are getting stronger, have better vascular tone and feel better overall. But, interestingly enough, your body weight may not have changed at all! In fact, it could even have *increased* through this process, because muscle is heavier than fat—but you would have achieved a higher level of fitness.

Likewise, many organizations want to have a profitable year but find that profitability is hard to measure and difficult to attain, so they focus on other things, such as revenue, acquiring new customers, or improving quality. These are all good and important performance drivers, but not necessarily key indicators of profits.

A telecommunications call center was having trouble with caller satisfaction due to long wait times, often going over twenty minutes. They had hired more employees to address the incoming calls, but the wait times were not significantly decreasing. They conducted training, and wait times remained the same. When I was called in to consult with the company, I noticed that screens everywhere around the call center displayed the number of callers in the queue with the names of the employees who were actively engaged in calls. This motivated employees to keep their names up on the display as engaged in customer conversations. Once a conversation was done, employees would pick up the next waiting caller immediately. So, average wait times remained high.

We decided to change the display to show *target* versus actual wait times per employee—a goal orientation, instead of an activity orientation. Red, yellow, and green color codes highlighted each person's status relative to the goal. Employees very quickly adjusted their behavior to bring their numbers into green, at or above the goal. They even started competing with other employees for best average times. Wait times went down immediately—even when the number of employees making calls was reduced! This is the power of goal orientation versus activity orientation.

WINNING AT THE GAME OF WORK

People naturally want to succeed. In life, in sports, and at work, everyone wants to win. So as a strategic execution leader, you can create the rules of the game and set up the scoreboard to help employees win by doing what helps the organization win too. The genius is to align the measurements and make them visible so everyone can win at the game of work.

How you set the rules of the game matters. Start by defining the proper goal. Set a measurable target that defines success for the organization. Make a clear connection between the organization's success and everyone's success in the organization. For example, achieving a set profit target means everyone keeps their job and receives a meaningful profit-sharing bonus. Keep the formula super simple so people can easily calculate what share of profits they will get.

Then set a scoreboard that shows how the organization is doing on a regular basis. This needs to be visually available to everyone in the organization, even if it is a confidential scoreboard. Help each team identify tangible ways they can contribute to the goal and, if possible, track their contributions at the team or individual level. Individuals need to know how they are contributing to the goal on a regular basis so they can adjust their behavior to succeed.

Let the game of work begin! Keep it simple. Make it fun. Recognize effort. Celebrate wins. Reward goal achievement. Most people will naturally do their best to succeed. Make sure that there is plenty of encouragement for all, even as some individuals do better than others. A healthy dose of competitive spirit is fine, as long as the competitive focus remains on the performance of individuals and not on the individuals themselves. The idea is to help everyone be able to succeed.

* * *

The game of work became a tangible concept as I was having lunch with James, a top sales professional at a fast-growing company that had just received an excellence award. I had known James since he started working at this company. James wanted to succeed at his job; he was an eager learner, trying to absorb everything he could about the customers and products and services the company offered.

Early in his career, he was part of a sales team that was struggling to establish a reliable sales process and deliver a consistent revenue goal. Several sales professionals had come on board but left after a few months of disappointing results. The sales team was demotivated and under pressure to perform. That's when James decided to start the game of work.

James asked senior management to put up a prize for hitting the sales goal for the quarter, and he was given a dollar amount he could use for the prize. Then he placed on a wall, in front of the entire sales team, a picture of a Jamaican ocean beach with the sales goal written over it.

He announced to his teammates that at least one of them was going to go on a five-day vacation to Jamaica at the end of the quarter. He didn't know who in the team would win the contest—it could even be him—but he was going to make sure that at least one of them won. All they needed to do was to hit the sales team goal, and the top seller for the quarter would go.

Everyone was stunned and excited by the proposal. The picture of the Jamaican ocean beach next to the number was a powerful motivator. The team wrote down the names of each salesperson on a whiteboard with a number next to each name representing their individual sales goal. Everyone aimed high so they could be the winner of the Jamaican trip, but the most important point was that the sum total for the team would exceed the team goal for the quarter. Game on!

As the days went by, each person updated the whiteboard with their actual sales. A healthy spirit of competition drove each person to do their very best. Some came in earlier to start working on the East Coast clients. Others worked at their desk during lunch. Everyone wanted to listen to each other's pitches on the phone so they could pick up the best phrases for selling. They asked to have sales training sessions once a week before the workday started. The team was on fire.

Before the end of the quarter, they had achieved the sales goal. Now it was a matter of who would win the trip to Jamaica. There were three top contenders for the prize. It was a close competition to the last day of the quarter, and, in the end, James won. As senior management recognized the entire sales team for a stellar quarter and honored James with the award, he asked that the award be placed in a draw for anyone in the team to get. That showed remarkable team spirit from one of the youngest teammates.

Fast forward ten years. Now, James was sitting right in front of me at the lunch table as the vice president of sales and marketing for one of the top companies in the industry. He had built a high-performing sales team that had just received one of the highest awards for sales excellence. He was invited to come to New York City to receive the award at a gala event. But he asked that the award be mailed to them, since everyone in the team was too busy selling to go to the event.

Right then, as we were about to finish our lunch interview, James got a call. He excused himself to take it. I listened to James while finishing my lunch. When he was done with the call, James told me it was a call from the office. "I'm sorry," he said, "I have to leave you now. It's the last day of the quarter. We are still a few thousand dollars short of our team sales goal. The entire team will go on a cruise to Mexico with our spouses if we make our goal. The boat and the flights are reserved already, so I need to go to help my team meet their goal."

James left the restaurant, his lunch unfinished, his personal goal met, but on his way to ensure that the entire team, now counting over a dozen members, would be able to enjoy the taste of winning the game of work.

* * *

If you want to achieve results, set a goal. Stop reporting on activities completed. Measure the performance that helps you reach the goal. What is measured gets attention. What is reported improves. The reporting frequency sets the pace for improvement. Reporting results on a scorecard starts the game of work. And have fun!

KEY TAKEAWAYS

- To deliver results, you must focus on *results*, not *activities*.
- What you measure is what you get. Change the measurement and you immediately change the results.
- A results-driven improvement process sees success as an ongoing series of incremental, measurable improvements, and focuses on the specific things people need to do to directly achieve results.
- If you are results oriented, your focus will be to:
  - Set effective goals
  - Measure key indicators
  - Improve performance
  - Report achievements
  - Analyze actual results versus goal results

- A goal should be a measurable, defined, long-term achievement. It has to have a number attached to it—if it doesn't, it is probably not a measurable achievement. Neither a vision nor an initiative nor an objective is a goal.
- What is measured and reported gets everyone's attention and therefore improves those areas. And the frequency of the reporting sets the pace for that improvement.

CHAPTER ELEVEN

DRIVE VALUE— DELIVERING WHAT MATTERS MOST

The ultimate goal for strategic transformation is to create value. Value creation is the natural result of converting inputs into useful outputs through intelligent labor. The transformational leader is motivated by creating value.

But what exactly is value creation? People create value in countless ways. Value creation is the natural outcome when people's talents are applied to good purposes. However, value isn't *inevitably* created through labor. When labor is applied incorrectly, without intelligence, it misuses input, resulting in negative output—value destruction. For example, selfish or thoughtless actions can result in value destruction.

The strategic transformation leader creates value by optimizing the organization's capacity for intelligent work. This requires three key components. First, the strategy. It is critical to have a clear plan to position your company for success. Then you need the strategic transformation process to implement that plan in a way that starts delivering what matters most. The final component is the value creation that is the result of the first two when they produce results.

The Strategic Transformation Framework describes how this is to be done, step by step:

1. Define a strategy that creates value

2. To implement a strategy, a leader does the following:

    - Builds common purpose through vision

    - Creates clarity through focus

    - Builds the right talent set by developing or hiring the right people

    - Aligns people to an effective organizational structure

    - Streamlines work through intelligent processes

    - Accelerates execution using agile processes

    - Brings out the best in others through engagement with them

    - Reports results achievement by measuring performance

3. Create value by attracting investment opportunities

From Here . . . ⬅▭ STRATEGIC TRANSFORMATION ▭▭▷ To There!

RED FRAME of MIND		GREEN FRAME of MIND
• Stuck by current state	1. Define a strategy that creates value	• Create the future state
• This is happening to me	2. Implement strategic transformation	• I'm making decisions
• Limited opportunities	3. Create value by attracting investment	• Make new opportunities

Figure 11.1

The strategic transformation process takes an organization from its current state to the desired future state. Strategic transformation leaders start by capturing the vision themselves and then getting others to help transform the organization. As they start generating positive momentum, they realize early wins that can be leveraged into more substantial gains to accelerate value creation. The uptick in performance that points to promising projections attracts new investment opportunities.

The strategic leader needs to determine what type of value is most needed at a given time. It may be strategic, financial, investment, or social value. Each requires a different approach.

Ultimately, value is in the eyes of the beholder. For this reason, the strategic leader needs to determine what type of value is most needed at a given time. It may be strategic, financial, investment, or social value. Each requires a different approach. Depending on the situation, a strategic transformation leader may need to prioritize one type of enterprise value over another.

A leader creates *strategic value* by developing products, services, customers, access to markets, or core capabilities that are unique, exclusive, or difficult to reproduce by competitors. This makes the enterprise very attractive to other companies in the industry. Pursuing strategic value requires intelligent market positioning.

A leader creates *financial value* by establishing dependable profits and reliable growth projections. This makes the company very attractive to financial partners seeking a defined return on investment. Going after financial value requires strong capital management.

A leader creates *investment value* by delivering predictable and steady returns for shareholders. This makes the company a sound business investment in the long run, creating stable economic value. Delivering solid shareholder value requires strong operational management.

A leader creates *social value* by developing dependable jobs, customer loyalty, and public confidence in the company's brand promise. This makes the company an asset to a community.

If the purpose of an enterprise is to create value through intelligent labor, then the enterprise value is determined when there is a buyer. Until that point, an organization is building its value over time. It is in the buy–sell exchange that the enterprise value becomes fully realized.

The reasons a buyer buys an enterprise are usually different from the reasons a seller sells an enterprise. Understanding the basic reasons and subtle motivations of buyers and sellers opens important possibilities in establishing a fair market value. In preparing for the sale of a company, it is wise for the seller and the advisor to conduct a valuation analysis from the buyer's perspective. This analysis may uncover value points that are important to the buyer but might be overlooked by the seller.

For example, financial buyers typically want to know that customers will stay around for a long time. They want assurances about future cash flow and stability of income, whereas strategic buyers are often looking to gain access to a set of customers they haven't been able to reach. They want to know specifically what types of relationships and contacts the company has with specific customers. The seller, on the other hand, may want to reduce personal exposure to debt or start an exit from the business. Understanding these motives is critical to optimizing the value during the transaction.

Nonbuyers also value the enterprise in different ways. Shareholders want to keep the company producing a stable income, customers want the company to keep delivering quality goods or services, and employees want to retain stable and lucrative employment. A smart leader takes into consideration the needs of these groups, too, because their loyalty adds to the value of the company.

* * *

In 1997, after just three years in business, an online book seller filed for an initial public offering. Facing stiff competition from established book sellers such as Simon & Schuster and Barnes & Noble, each of which was already selling books online, the company stock listed at $18 per share on IPO day.

Jeff Bezos drew up the business plan for Amazon while on a road trip from New York to Seattle. With an investment from his parents, Bezos left his job at D. E. Shaw to start Amazon from his garage. Amazon had no clear path to profitability, and it took a long time before it started making money.

For many years, investors were nervous about the stock and pressured Bezos to push for profits. Amazon was growing fast, but it was producing losses of increasing magnitude. Bezos wanted to expand into other products besides books. He insisted that Amazon needed to achieve its full size and market penetration before producing profits.

For a while, Amazon's decision to favor growth over profits was very controversial. Investors were getting impatient; many considered selling and many actually left. Bezos knew that realizing his vision for Amazon would take a long time, but that, when it did happen, the profit would be enormous.

Those who stayed with Amazon saw the value of their investment rise five hundred times. They also became shareholders of one of the world's dominant online marketplaces. To illustrate what this means, $1,000 invested at the closing price on Amazon's IPO day would be worth nearly half a million dollars twenty years later. That kind of return escaped even the most seasoned investors. Warren Buffett, Berkshire Hathaway CEO, would admit that he was "too dumb to realize what was going to happen."

In business, what's dangerous is not to evolve.

—*Jeff Bezos*

THE DRIVERS THAT DETERMINE VALUE

As a strategic transformation leader, you need to understand where the value of your organization lies, because it is in realizing that value that the enterprise becomes valuable to others. From the seller's point of view, the key to successful value exchange is preparation. For the buyer, the emphasis is on thorough analysis of multiple opportunities and due diligence.

As a strategic transformation leader, you need to understand where the value of your organization lies, because it is in realizing that value that the enterprise becomes valuable to others.

While there are multiple factors affecting your company's value, the four main value drivers are:

- Income (profits)

- Growth (revenues)

- Market comparisons (multiples)

- Resources (net assets)

INCOME DRIVERS

The amount of cash a business can generate in the future is one of the most important drivers for enterprise value. Companies generating predictable profits command a premium by estimating the present value of future projected income. Since there is always some uncertainty about future performance, you must include a risk factor when you project cash flows over the next three to five years. You can estimate the enterprise's current value by projecting the net present value of future cash flows. This is called the Discounted Cash Flows (DCF) valuation method.

GROWTH DRIVERS

For companies that are growing at a rapid rate but are not yet producing profits at all or not at the target levels, it is best to estimate value based on revenue projections that show strong growth. The idea is that a fast-growing company will at some point start realizing profits. Investors looking at the long-term value of the company will pay attention to annual revenues, revenue growth rate year over year, and projected profit margins at a mature stage. This valuation is typically based on applying a multiple to annual revenues determined by the growth rate. For example, a multiple of one time the revenue means that the company is worth as much as it is currently making in annual sales. If projections show a strong growth rate, the multiple can be two, four, or even six times the current revenue.

MARKET DRIVERS

A company can be valued based on the price for which similar companies have been sold and purchased. For publicly traded companies, that value is determined by the stock price. For a private enterprise, this requires an analysis of recent market transactions. It is often difficult to establish exact peer-to-peer comparisons, but by establishing comparable transactions in the industry, you can estimate a reasonable market price range and median valuation point. To facilitate comparisons across companies of different sizes, prices are established as a multiple of revenues and earnings before interest, taxes, depreciation, and amortization (EBITDA).

Companies tend to trade within their industry multiples. Certain industries tend to have a higher multiplier range, based on how fast the industry is growing. So, for example, in recent times, technology—especially innovative software technology—has been commanding a premium. Other industries with less growth potential trade at smaller multiples. Multiples favor larger companies, as they usually present greater market opportunities and fewer risks than smaller ones. This causes smaller companies to become attractive to larger ones, as the buyer can immediately increase their value due to a higher multiple.

RESOURCES DRIVERS

For companies that have invested heavily in infrastructure, equipment, and inventory, valuation can be based on the market value of the assets minus liabilities. This is called the asset value of the business and includes both tangible and intangible elements. Assets such as intellectual property, know-how, patents, and leadership experience become a valuable asset. Likewise, intangible liabilities such as geo-political risk or pending lawsuits can be taken into account.

Tesla is an example of this, as Tesla's supply and manufacturing system was very expensive to build. For a long time, Tesla has been undervalued, because there were no profits and a huge up-front investment in infrastructure. When the infrastructure was in place and investors saw that it could be scaled to produce enough of the company's innovative products, the value of Tesla sharply increased.

Using multiple valuation methods helps buyers and sellers determine a fair market value. These parameters serve as general guidelines to establish the enterprise value range. Negotiations usually happen within the range established by these valuation parameters.

Ultimately, the value of an enterprise is determined by what price a buyer is willing to pay for it and what price a seller is willing to accept for it. By engaging multiple potential buyers, the seller is more likely to receive the maximum price. On the other hand, when buyers can consider multiple options, they can make the best investment decision. For this purpose, we strongly recommend going through a competitive bidding process to obtain optimal terms and price.

Understanding the valuation drivers helps you, as the leader, conduct a strategic transformation to position your company to create and attract maximum value.

* * *

I worked with a technology firm that had a very innovative value proposition for personalized online marketing based on mining customer profiles. Such an approach was new at the time, and this company was one of the early players. They had several rounds of investment, each bringing in additional capital to the company, and they were expecting to raise new capital every two years. The company was intentionally not trying to produce a profit, but instead was spending all that capital to create the fastest possible growth in the market by delivering the most innovative product.

The company was attracting some of the smartest and brightest software engineers available, because it was being very aggressive about innovation. They were constantly posting hacker forums and think labs and innovation forums, bringing in experts on artificial intelligence, machine learning, big data analytics, and so on.

Their sales team was going after very large organizations, letting those organizations use the product in the beta stage free of charge—even for years after the company could have monetized the software. The idea was that if renowned companies were using their technology, then many other companies would follow suit and pay full price for the product.

So this company was spending money constantly, at a very accelerated rate, but investors were still eager to give them *more* money so the investors could benefit from the future success of this technology.

The leaders of the company understood their position in the market and focused their execution on growth drivers, because it was the values of growth and future profits that investors were looking at when valuing the company.

The following lists serve as a general guide to what buyers tend to consider the most important valuation parameters:

PRIMARY DRIVERS OF VALUATION:

- Historical and projected EBITDA
- Annual revenue amount
- Historical and projected revenue stability
- Profit margins
- Return on assets
- Growth potential
- Market size and trends
- Customer concentrations

SECONDARY DRIVERS OF VALUATION:

- Financial controls
- Asset quality
- Revenue concentration
- Competitive landscape
- Management team
- Staffing levels

- Material & equipment demands
- Quality control
- Facilities
- Regulatory issues

OTHER POTENTIAL DRIVERS OF VALUATIONS:

- Employee turnover
- Training
- Local talent pool
- Operations systems
- Payroll as percent of sales
- Legal issues
- Certifications & licenses

CAPITAL STRATEGIES TO CREATE VALUE

Successful entrepreneurs are constantly dealing with two issues: how to make more money and what to do with the money they've already made. While good options abound, good choices are unusual. Brilliant financial allocation decisions are scarce, even for the best and brightest, and for a good reason.

All too often, entrepreneurs rely on their instincts to make business decisions without assessing the value of previous choices. This is understandable, because they are confident that what got them where they *are* will take them where they *want to go*. Familiarity with an approach and a natural skill set tend to drive their business decisions more than sound thinking, so many entrepreneurs keep doing what they've been doing without fully evaluating the results of their previous choices in light of their future needs.

All too often, entrepreneurs rely on their instincts to make business decisions without assessing the value of previous choices.

In addition, without a proper assessment of the strategies best suited for a business, growth tactics can lack true innovative thinking and become a reiteration of past strategies. Others may commit to entirely new strategies more on their gut feel for it than on any evidence that it will bring success.

To address these concerns, study the following seven strategies to determine the best ones to help you grow your business.

1. MINIMAL VALUE CASH INVESTMENT

The simplest and safest approach to creating wealth from an idea is to try it with a minimal cash investment. That's how most entrepreneurs start their careers. Even in more mature businesses, testing a new approach works best when using the same approach as a start-up. Avoid the temptation to supercharge the start-up with resources that will be consumed before the idea is fully vetted. Instead, focus on business fundamentals. Offer a minimal value product or service with a minimal cash investment. Work to obtain a return and then reinvest the proceeds to keep growing the return incrementally.

A cosmetic contract manufacturer start-up went into business with limited seed capital which required lots of hard work, long hours, and dedication by the original core team. Limited resources sparked the spirit of resourcefulness and innovation. To win customers, they lowered barriers to entry by offering discounts on product development and reduced minimum quantity orders. As the initial smaller accounts grew into larger ones, the owners decided to reinvest their profits to fund future growth.

2. SELF-FINANCING GROWTH

As a business starts growing, there is usually a need for additional capital. The least expensive capital is your own, so some entrepreneurs choose to bootstrap. By keeping costs to a minimum and aggressively pursuing sales, some businesses manage to self-finance their growth from cash flow. Gross margins, payment cycles, and growth rate are critical for determining if this approach will be sustainable. By paying close attention to cash flows, you can manage to successfully grow your business debt free and keep control of how and when you grow on your own. If this is your situation, congratulations!

3. GROWTH INVESTMENT

Often self-funding can limit more ambitious growth opportunities. Besides, some business concepts have to scale fast or become prey to others. This requires capital to accelerate growth. Growth capital usually comes from two sources: debt or equity, or a mix of the two. Debt capital is less expensive in the long run, but places a burden on the business and a personal liability on the entrepreneur. Equity capital comes at a long-term cost, but could bring in critical funding and valuable partners to the business. Keep in mind that the intelligence, experience, and resources that these new partners bring to the table can be just as valuable as their capital. A mix of these two approaches can offset the risks and benefits of each approach. Consider this strategy when scalability is critical and you are highly confident about successful growth if you get a capital infusion.

4. CAPACITY BUILDING

Once a business is more mature and organic growth is predictable, further growth can come from increasing market share. This requires reinvesting a portion of existing and projected profits in capacity building. Managing future cash flow allows a business to fund growth by building a stronger infrastructure. The investment should be managed to generate predictable returns within a sustainable cash flow cycle. A line of credit or other forms of short-term debt are the best ways to provide a shock absorber to fund the expansion.

5. DIVERSIFIED REVENUE STREAMS

If a business's product lines or service offerings are becoming so mature that growth is slowing down or even declining, it is time to diversify. Some entrepreneurs foresee the trend ahead of the competition and start diversifying early on. This move, if done successfully, can turn them into an industry innovator or disruptor. Successful diversification requires significant strategic foresight, as you need to bet on where the market is going. Diversification is best pursued through self-financing growth, strategic partnerships, joint ventures, and/or mergers and acquisitions. Which approach is best for you depends on clear strategic thinking.

The cosmetic contract manufacturing firm I mentioned earlier recognized the need to diversify revenue streams early. To expand services, they offered clients an end-to-end turnkey process from product formulation to marketing, production, and fulfillment. This one-stop shop approach attracted larger contracts and deeper partnerships. It resulted in several clients becoming joint ventures that expanded the revenue streams.

6. STRATEGIC PARTNERSHIPS AND JOINT VENTURES

Strategic partnerships and joint ventures allow you to share the risk and the rewards with a partner that brings in a new and attractive set of competencies. Engaging in a partnership implies that the main business is willing to invest a discrete amount of time, money, and expertise on a person or a group that brings a new and complementary set of resources or capabilities not available internally. There is usually a time required to prove the concept before the parties are vested in the partnership. Partnerships can be structured with cash only or cash and equity incentives. A joint venture is a partnership where both parties retain their distinct businesses and join up as limited partners for a specific venture.

The cosmetic contract manufacturer decided to further expand growth opportunities by establishing select joint ventures. The owners decided to defer research and development, branding, and packaging design costs for select high-potential clients in return for equity in their business or a share of profits. Those entrepreneurial companies immediately saw the value of reducing up-front costs and became joint ventures. Leveraging each company's strengths gives the joint venture a unique set of capabilities that would otherwise be too expensive to build.

7. MERGERS AND ACQUISITIONS

When there is a need to deliver significant growth and ample financial resources are available, pursuing growth through acquisitions can prove the fastest way to achieve the goal. Acquisitions can bring in an existing business and an entirely new portfolio of products, services, and customers. If structured correctly, an acquisition can create a financial event to help capitalize the seller and the buyer. Special attention needs to be paid to merging organizational cultures and the ability to manage the acquired business successfully after the transaction. A company can also seek to be acquired, if its leaders feel that they have achieved their goals and want to capitalize on what they've created.

BUILD, BUY, OR PARTNER

Cisco Systems is a prime example of growth through acquisitions, counting more than two hundred acquisitions in its history. Founded in 1984 by a husband-and-wife team of Stanford University computer scientists, Cisco competed in the rapidly emerging networking connectivity market. To remain at the leading edge of innovation, Cisco Systems' chairman and CEO, John Chambers, set out to buy what he could not develop quickly enough.

For the first ten years, the company's fortunes were almost exclusively tied to their core product—the router. The advent of the internet drove the need for supplying a complex array of technologies well beyond what Cisco could hope to develop internally. To stay out in front of the relentless pace of innovation, Cisco became a savvy acquirer of innovative tech firms through simple and friendly deals.

At a Cisco management conference I attended as a consultant, Mr. Chambers welcomed the several hundred participants by recognizing the various companies represented besides Cisco. Many in the room worked at start-ups aspiring to become part of Cisco, and some could be potential competitors. Mr. Chambers acknowledged that everyone had been invited to be part of a remarkable undertaking: to build the largest network in the history of mankind. He set the tone for the rest of the event by stating that it would take everyone's best thinking and hardest work to build the infrastructure for the internet. He indicated that those with the best complementary solutions would be welcome to join Cisco, and those who chose to compete would do well to be aware of where to go.

Cisco's acquisition strategy became an integral part of the company's culture. The acquisition process evolved into a blueprint for every newly acquired company to be smoothly shipping their products under the Cisco label by the time the deal was closed, usually within three to six months of the initial interaction. Start-up owners were given executive roles at Cisco and ample freedom to pursue their goals, fueled by larger resources.

Driven to accelerate time to market, Cisco has made a few mistakes along the way, with the prevailing view that "if we are not making mistakes, we aren't moving fast enough." The two keys to a successful acquisition, according to Cisco management, are doing the homework to select the right company and applying an effective and replicable integration process once the deal is struck.

Pursuing acquisitions has propelled Cisco Systems' growth. Understanding your own situation and deciding on your organization's best strategies will help you create value by building a successful business. Making the right choices—choosing the right kind of strategic transformation—will help you accelerate growth.

KEY TAKEAWAYS

- The ultimate goal for the strategic transformation of any organizational strategy is to create value—the natural result of transforming input into useful output through intelligent labor.
- The strategic transformation leader creates value by optimizing the organization's capacity for intelligent work.
- There are four main value drivers for an enterprise:
  - Income (profits)
  - Growth (revenues)
  - Market comparisons (multiples)
  - Resources (net assets)
- The primary drivers of valuation are:
  - Historical and projected EBITDA
  - Annual revenue amount
  - Historical and projected revenue stability
  - Profit margins
  - Return on assets
  - Growth potential
  - Market size and trends
  - Customer concentrations
- There are seven strategies to choose from to help you grow your business:
  - Minimal cash investment
  - Self-financing growth
  - Growth investment
  - Capacity building
  - Diversified revenue streams
  - Strategic partnerships and joint ventures
  - Mergers and acquisitions

CHAPTER TWELVE

LEADERSHIP—TAKING ORGANIZATIONS TO THE NEXT LEVEL

We live in a world of accelerating change. But not all change succeeds. How can you tell if the change your organization is pursuing will succeed or fail?

If you knew what to look for, you could predict the likely outcome of your initiative and, if necessary, make a course correction. This single, valuable insight could save you a great deal of frustration and painful loss. But you *don't* know the likely outcome, so the challenge is knowing how to thrive in an uncertain world of accelerating change. In today's fast-changing environment, success depends on your ability to learn and adapt quickly.

In an uncertain world of accelerating change success depends on your ability to learn and adapt quickly.

People say that change is the constant. But change no longer happens at a constant pace—it's accelerating! For several decades now, we have been experiencing this accelerating pace of change. The business climate is punctuated with amazing highs and sharp lows. We experience incredible threats as well as remarkable opportunities.

The driving forces for change are many. To name just a few, we live in a world of technological disruption (the main driving force), political instability, economic uncertainty, information explosion, shifting social norms, cultural tensions, massive migrations, and unprecedented climate change. The traditional patterns that delivered tried-and-true results often don't work anymore.

It's as if there's a new playbook out there, but new pages keep getting added all the time, the rules keep changing. Ironically, we have more data available from more sources than ever before in history, yet we lack predictability. It's more difficult than ever to find a clear direction.

Business strategies that used to set a course for five to ten years these days barely stay on course for a year. While on one hand, corporations are leveraging big changes such as artificial intelligence to optimize marketing decisions, on the other hand, they are dumbfounded by the changes caused by constant market disruption.

For the last several decades, we have been experiencing exponential change on many fronts. Our world is evolving faster than in previous centuries—and even in recent decades. Where is this all headed? No one really knows. But what we do know for sure is that, for better or worse, change is happening, more frequently and dramatically, right before our eyes and at our fingertips, as we are both the spectators and the actors in this historical shift. We experience the anxiety and uncertainties as well as the excitement and opportunities. We both *cause* our accelerating times and experience the *effects* of this acceleration.

BET ON THE FUTURE

Your challenge as the strategic transformation leader is to take your organization to the next level in this world of rapid change. Your task is to inspire commitment, set a clear direction, empower the right people, foster collaboration, and deliver critical results—even if, at times, you feel inadequate to the task.

As a leader, you are the person who really makes things happen. You have ideas, people, processes, and tools to make those things happen. Others stand by ready to assist you. This book lays out for you the path forward. But you are still the catalyst for the strategic transformation. Your decisions and approach set the course. Are you leading strategic change or just reacting to financial and political pressures?

Every person, team, and organization is somewhere along a continuum between simply reacting to change and leading change. Where are you, your team, and your organization on that continuum? More importantly, what approach are you taking? Are you reacting to, responding to, or leading change? Reacting to change does not produce a transformation. Leading change takes people to the next level.

Your answer determines how you will fare in today's environment. From evolutionary science, we learn that it is not the strongest species that survives, nor the most intelligent, but the one *most responsive to change*. In this context, let's review the likely outcome of your attempt to transform your organization, based on each different approach to dealing with change.

It is not the strongest species that survives, nor the most intelligent, but the one most responsive to change.

REACTING TO CHANGE

Many people and organizations are barely able to react to the external forces shaping their industries. They *are* changing, but slower than the external environment. They play it safe, taking minimal risks, because they're afraid of the uncertainty out there. Playing it safe has some benefits, such as learning from others' mistakes. But, most often, this risk-averse approach results in not learning fast enough, so these organizations become less competitive and less relevant over time. At some point, they may go out of business, because their competition has exceeded them in the market.

ADAPTING TO CHANGE

Most organizations are actively managing to keep up with changing trends. They are responding and adapting to the changing landscape—not with a game changing approach, but simply by seeing what others are doing and continuing to make the incremental changes that keep them in the game. They manage to remain viable as their industries change. Proactively responding to change is a strategy for staying in the game, but not for winning the game. These organizations tend to grow at the industry's pace, riding the ups and downs of the economy, but not in any way taking advantage of, or benefiting from, the fast-changing environment they're in.

LEADING CHANGE

Fewer are the organizations that thrive in turbulent times, not only changing with the times but also defining the future and learning how to profit from the changes it will bring. These organizations shape their industries, advance innovative ideas, and create aspects of the future that we will all live in.

There are definitely risks involved in doing this, but being a true leader means taking risks in order to seize opportunities—and seizing opportunities will teach an organization important lessons, even if a particular opportunity fails. These organizations learn fast from failed opportunities, recover quickly and, ultimately, because of what they learn, end up defining more optimal models for succeeding in the emerging environment. Because these organizations move faster than the pace of external change, they become the innovators, the pace setters, the ones that everyone else follows.

Organizations that change slower than the external pace of change fall behind and become less relevant. Organizations that innovate experience growth, gain an advantage, and take the lead. How does your organization respond to a changing world?

Organizations that innovate experience growth, gain an advantage, and take the lead.

---

* * *

After receiving news of the market crash that began the Great Depression, John D. Rockefeller made one of the biggest business bets in history. He had started a monumental real estate development project in the heart of Manhattan, to be called Rockefeller Center. "It was clear that there were only two courses open to me," Rockefeller later said. "One was to abandon the entire development. The other was to go forward with it in the definite knowledge that I myself would have to build it and finance it alone."

Was it worth the risk? With the huge economic downturn, there was a growing surplus of vacant real estate in the city and Rockefeller had no foreseeable tenants for his new development. But he believed that if he created something unique and attractive, the development would ultimately prosper. He decided to push ahead as the sole financial backer of the biggest office development project in history. Building this colossal edifice gave thousands of people jobs and hope through those grim times. And Rockefeller did not cut corners on the project. He insisted on having the highest-quality design, construction, and décor.

Ultimately, Rockefeller's innovative development attracted the headquarters of an emerging—and ultimately burgeoning—technology: radio. Thus, "30 Rock" became the broadcasting heart of the American mass media industry. Today, Rockefeller Center stands as a symbol of betting on the future, demonstrating the kind of risk creative leaders take to prosper even in uncertain times.

WRESTLING THE FIVE HUNDRED-POUND GORILLA

Heavyweight boxing champion Mike Tyson once said, "Everyone has a plan, till they get punched in the mouth." When dealing with strategic change, leaders sometimes face huge, daunting challenges that test their mettle. They have a plan and think they know what they're doing, but then something huge and unexpected happens and they are daunted or even overwhelmed by the situation. It's as if they've suddenly come face to face with a five hundred-pound gorilla and feel totally outmatched and inadequate.

When faced with that five hundred-pound gorilla, you need to get into action quickly. You can't reason with the gorilla. You can't outrun it. You need to face it and do something, then and there. For your change to succeed, you need to be ready to encounter, deal with, and tame the five hundred-pound gorillas when they appear. Are there five hundred-pound gorillas you need to deal with in your organization? Are there ones lurking in the world that might affect your strategic transformation plan?

Over the last few decades, there have been a growing number of five hundred-pound-gorilla-sized crises. Some have played out on a global scale, affecting organizations all over the world, while others dramatically affected certain industries or kinds of companies: the Y2K computer update scare; the terrorist attacks of September 11, 2001; Enron's scandal supported by the accounting fraud of accounting firm Arthur Anderson; an international financial crisis with a corresponding massive bailout package in the USA; numerous viral infectious diseases—COVID-19 being the latest—and earthquakes, floods, and tsunamis.

Facing situations like these, leaders at all levels are often puzzled or overwhelmed by what feels like the engulfing doom of the situation.

But people need leadership to know how to deal with these crises. Pressure mounts on the leader to respond, to set a direction and act appropriately. As a strategic transformation leader, do you know what to do? And more importantly, are you proactively leading?

By studying the decisions made by effective leaders under these kinds of circumstances, we can discern a distinctive pattern that, if followed, will produce the best short-term results and that will stand as a lasting and sustainable path forward in the long run. I'll describe that pattern in terms of a metaphor I used when responding to a client alarmed by the effect of the COVID-19 virus shutdown on his fast-growing marketing agency.

All of this entrepreneur's workers had been sent home. All of his customers were also working from home and trying to decide whether they would continue to do business with him in their circumstances. They were asking for concessions in their contracts and terms of service. If they couldn't get them, they would have to look into canceling their contracts with his company. "What do I do?" he asked, a tone of desperation in his voice.

"Imagine yourself as a race car driver approaching a tight, unexpected turn," I told him. "This is a critical time, when your performance will determine whether you stay on the road, skid off and crash, or, at least, lose or gain positions in the race."

He said, "Yeah, that's exactly what this is like. I don't even know how long this turn will be—or if there are three more tight turns ahead, but all I know is that I feel these big forces pushing against me."

"So as you're going into this tight corner," I said, "touch the brakes a little. This reduces your speed so you can maintain control of your car. This means you might have to enact some light measures to reduce unnecessary costs and conserve your cash. If there is something that is not essential, that won't cut into the core of your business, this is the time to defund that. This will help keep you stable, help you keep control of your business.

"Then, as you make the turn, hold on tight, because multiple forces will be pressing the car to make it go out of control. Stay on track as you make the turn. This means you should find opportunities to stay as close to your plan as you can, to do things to keep you on track as much as possible.

"As you start to complete this dangerous turn, respond decisively—shift into a higher gear and accelerate out of the turn. This means you need to be ready to make investments in the future, in strategic areas that you foresee being important opportunities for growing your company."

I've seen this approach to dealing with a crisis situation work time and time again. Not giving up on the business, but pulling back enough to keep control and accelerating your activity as you start coming out of the crisis, so when you are out of the crisis you're in a strong position, going at full speed. It's a bet on your future!

* * *

> *Kites rise highest against the wind, not with it.*
>
> —*Winston Churchill*

England was facing annihilation. The Nazis had conquered most of Europe—including pushing the British army out of France and nearly destroying it at Dunkirk. Hitler was gathering troops, ships, and planes along the coast of France, just twenty-one miles from England. It looked as if the island nation that ruled one-fourth of the world's population was about to fall—like Poland, Czechoslovakia, France, Belgium, the Netherlands, Norway, and Sweden had fallen before the Nazi *blitzkrieg*. The situation was desperate.

Some people in England felt it was time to settle with Hitler, to make a peace that would prevent the invasion. But England was at war with the Nazis, and Prime Minister Winston Churchill was determined not to negotiate with a brutal dictator, not to cave in to Hitler. He turned to the United States of America for help. He and Franklin Roosevelt knew and respected each other. But Roosevelt was hamstrung by political considerations in a nation that was still too heavily isolationist and would not provide the help England needed.

So if England was to resist the Nazis, it would have to do that, for the time being, on its own. King George VI, England's monarch, met secretly with Churchill and asked him what he thought they should do. The pressure to save lives at the cost of freedom was enormous. The attack on England was imminent and would result, all feared, in its invasion.

In his darkest hours before addressing the parliament, and with a load of responsibility on his shoulders, Churchill insisted that they had to resist the evil of Nazism, whatever the cost, because there was no one else left who would do it. King George told Churchill that he supported that decision.

But if England was going to successfully resist a Nazi invasion, it would take every ounce of dedication and grit the English people had. And Churchill, as their leader, knew he had to inspire their full commitment, courage, and dedication. The morning after his meeting with the king, Churchill went on national radio and made one of the greatest speeches of all time, the one which promised that England would resist invasion and defeat everywhere and in every way:

Even though large tracts of Europe and many old and famous states have fallen or may fall into the grip of the Gestapo and all the odious apparatus of Nazi rule, we shall not flag or fail. We shall go on to the end, we shall fight in France, we shall fight on the seas and oceans, we shall fight with growing confidence and growing strength in the air, we shall defend our island, whatever the cost may be, we shall fight on the beaches, we shall fight on the landing grounds, we shall fight in the fields and in the streets, we shall fight in the hills; we shall never surrender.

Rallied by Churchill's words, England's brave fighter pilots eventually defeated the Nazi air force over England in what became known as the Battle of Britain. That victory prevented Hitler from achieving the air superiority he believed necessary to his success and forced him to call off the invasion. Ultimately, England emerged stronger out of the adversity of World War II.

As one poet put it, facing adversity with determination and courage turns into strength.

Good timber does not grow with ease,
the stronger the wind, the stronger the trees,
the further the sky, the greater the length,
the more the storm, the more the strength.

By sun and cold, by rain and snow,
In trees and men good timbers grow.

—excerpt from "Good Timber" by Douglas Malloch

MOVING ONWARD AND UPWARD

Change is inevitable. Growth is optional. Executing a strategic transformation starts by recognizing change as an opportunity, rather than a threat.

Our ability to change with changing times is vital to remaining relevant. However, there is more to success than merely changing for change's sake. Not all change results in progress. To change for the better we must improve, grow, learn, and do better.

Strategic transformation leaders apply a variety of approaches and practices for influencing positive change. The Strategic Transformation Framework presents the leader's tool kit—filled with principles, processes, and practices to help make your strategy work. But ultimately, it is you, the leader, who has to put it all together. You become the catalyst for change; you put it all in motion.

In the end, it is the success of your people that is your success. Leadership is not about you, but about the purpose you instill in others. Change needs to become part of who they are—to the extent that when the strategy succeeds, they feel as if they did it themselves. Because they own it, have made it theirs. So it no longer feels like change, but like a new standard, a new way of thinking and acting.

In the end, it is the success of your people that is your success.

Gandhi exhorted people to "be the change that you wish to see in the world," and that is the desire you need to inspire in your people for a successful strategic transformation.

KEY TAKEAWAYS

- In today's fast-changing environment, success depends on your ability to learn and adapt quickly.

- You have the ideas, processes, and tools laid out in this book to help you, but you, the leader, are an important catalyst for the successful achievement of a strategic transformation.

- There are three ways that an organization can respond to change: reacting, adapting, and leading. Those leading change set the new standards that others follow.

- Organizations that change slower than the external pace of change fall behind and become less relevant. Organizations that innovate experience growth, gain an advantage, and take the lead.

- Crises are going to happen, and people need a leader to get through them. The most effective approach is not giving up on the business, but pulling back enough to keep control and preparing to accelerate your investment as you are coming out of the crisis.

- Leadership is about inspiring those you lead to reach their full potential.